MW01296987

This book is not intenc
biography of the people
you the basics of each ....,
hopefully, will encourage you to look deeper into the
lives of these wonderful individuals, many of whom
risked injury or death standing up for what was, and
is, right. Too many lost their lives in the pursuit of
racial justice.

Sadly, too many are unfamiliar with black history, with
the trials and challenges those who came before
endured. From slavery, to segregation to Jim Crow
laws to abuse by radical groups like the Ku Klux Klan
to ignorance, sometimes evidenced by the people we
elect to office.

Many people in this book endured the worst. Most of
them triumphed over the inequality and
discrimination to accomplish miracles. It is to them
this book is dedicated.

> A special thanks to my wife, Judi,
> for pushing me to finish this book
> and to my daughter Staci, the
> computer whiz, for re-doing it in
> the right format!!

Abraham Lincoln

Lincoln was born February 12, 1809 near Hodgenville, Kentucky.

He may have had little formal education but he was an avid reader and he was able to retain what he read.

His family eventually moved to Illinois where Lincoln found various jobs including captain in the state militia.

He met and married Mary Todd, the daughter of a wealthy slave owner on November 4, 1842. They had four children Edward Baker, Thomas "Tad," Willie and Robert Todd. Only Robert lived to adulthood. The deaths of their children affected both but especially Mary who suffered bouts of depression.

Lincoln became a lawyer, mostly self-taught, and entered the political arena running for the Illinois General Assembly. Lacking money and name recognition he lost. He finally was elected to the Illinois House of Representatives from the Whig Party where he served four terms.

In 1858, Senator Stephen Douglas, a Democrat, was up for re-election. Delegates at the Illinois Republican state convention chose Lincoln to oppose him. Seven debates followed, the major issue being slavery. Lincoln lost the election but gained national recognition. He became the Republican nominee for president two years later, a move which upset the southern states.

With his election as president 11 southern states seceded from the union which precipitated the civil war. On January 1, 1863 Lincoln gave a speech, the Emancipation Proclamation, which freed all slaves in the southern states. He was re-elected president in 1864.

On April 14, 1865 John Wilkes Booth shot Lincoln during a play at Ford's Theatre. The president died the following day.

Adam Clayton Powell Jr.

Powell was born November 29, 1908 in New Haven, Connecticut.

When his father became minister of the Abyssinian Baptist Church, the family moved to New York City then eventually to Harlem.

He was the assistant minister under his father and succeeded him in 1937. He immediately turned his attention to the needs of his community becoming an activist.

As his church began to grow, he felt empowered to demand more services, job opportunities and better housing for his parishioners.

In 1941 he entered the political arena winning a seat on the New York City Council, the first African-American elected. In 1945 he won election to the U.S. House of Representatives where he served for 24 years.

From the House floor he was able to speak out for human rights and against injustice. One of his campaigns was to make lynching a federal crime which became law a few years later.

He worked with the NAACP on many occasions and he proposed a bill denying federal assistance to any state which practiced segregation. It became part of the 1964 Civil Rights Act.

Advancing in Congress he became chairman of the Labor and Education Committee. They passed many pieces of legislation including the Minimum Wage Act, the Anti-Poverty Act and the formation of government sponsored and backed student loans, among others.

After his political career he retired to the island of Bimini in the Bahamas. His health deteriorated and he flew back to Miami for treatment where he died of acute prostatitis on April 4, 1972 at the age of 63.

Amelia Boynton Robinson

Robinson was born August 18, 1911 in Savannah, Georgia, one of 10 children.

Encouraged by her parents to read, she attended what is now Savannah State University before transferring to Tuskegee Institute. She graduated with a degree in home economics.

She taught school in Georgia and then moved to the U.S. Department of Agriculture becoming an agent who demonstrated the proper method of doing many household chores with a number of different household products.

In 1936 she wrote a play, *"Through the Years,"* the story of Robert Smalls (see his story in this book) as a fundraiser for one of her causes. During this time, she was also registering blacks to vote. Even as a young child she helped her mother advocate for women's suffrage.

In 1964 she ran for a seat in Congress from Alabama. She lost but her campaign spurred blacks to register to vote. After the election, she and other civil rights leaders began planning a march from Selma, Alabama to the state capital, Montgomery.

On March 7, 1965 more than 600 people, black and white, tried to cross the Edmund Pettis Bridge in Selma. Led by John Lewis, Hosea Williams and others, the marchers were met by 200 state troopers who used Billy clubs and tear gas to beat the marchers. Robinson was beaten unconscious. That day became known as "Bloody Sunday."

With Federal protection, 25,000 people made the march to Montgomery reaching the capital on March 24th.

Robinson was in the White House when President Johnson signed the Voting Rights Act of 1965. She received the Martin Luther King Jr. Freedom Medal in 1990. She died August 24, 2015 at 104.

Alvin Ailey, Jr.

Ailey was born in Rogers, Texas January 5, 1931. His father left the family when he was very young.

When his mother moved to California, Alvin joined the high school gymnastics team. His interest in dance grew when he began tap dancing lessons.

He joined Lester Horton's dance studio and learned many different styles of dance. When Horton died suddenly Ailey took over as artistic director and choreographer.

Some poor performance reviews resulted in the breakup of the group. Undeterred, Ailey began recruiting dancers for another troupe, the Alvin Ailey American Dance Theater.

The troupe was a gathering place for African-American dancers to perform during the time of segregation in America. At times, he also choreographed dance routines for other companies.

The U. S. State Department sent Ailey's dance troupes overseas as goodwill ambassadors. They danced in Asia and parts of Africa before returning home.

In 1969 he created the Alvin Ailey American Dance Center to give under-served communities access to dance. It's now the largest studio devoted to training dancers.

During a mental breakdown in 1980 he could no longer perform his duties so Judith Jamison, his leading dancer, took the helm.

Ailey received many awards for his dancing and choreography including the Spingarn Medal from the NAACP.

He died of AIDS related disease December 1, 1989.

Andrew Young

 Young was born March 12, 1932 in New Orleans, Louisiana. He attended segregated schools.

He graduated from Howard University, then received a degree in divinity before joining Bethany Congregational Church in Thomasville, Georgia as its pastor. The year was 1955.

While there Young became active in organizing voter registration drives.

In 1961 he went to work for the Southern Christian Leadership Conference then led by the Rev. Martin Luther King, Jr.

He eventually became executive director while continuing his efforts to register voters in Birmingham and Selma, Alabama.

After Dr. King was assassinated, Young turned to politics and in 1972 won Georgia's fifth congressional seat in the U. S. House of Representatives. He was the first African-American to represent Georgia in Congress since Reconstruction.

In 1977 President Jimmy Carter named him United States Ambassador to the United Nations where he made worldwide human rights his prime goal. He supported sanctions on South Africa in an effort to eliminate apartheid.

In 1981 he was elected mayor of Atlanta and he served two terms. He successfully brought the summer Olympic Games to Atlanta in1996 and served as co-chairman of the Atlanta Olympic Committee.

He's written a number of books and has received many awards for his civil rights activism.

Young has also taught at Georgia State University.

Arthur Ashe

Arthur Ashe was born July 10, 1943 in Richmond, Virginia.

Shortly after his mother's death he learned about a game called tennis

Loving the game, he caught the eye of Dr. Robert Johnson, Jr., a tennis coach who worked with Ashe to improve his game.

He was given a tennis scholarship to UCLA and while there was named to the 1963 U.S. Davis Cup team, the first African-American member. Two years later he won the NCAA singles and doubles championships.

After graduating UCLA, he served two years in the military.

While still an amateur he surprised everyone by winning the U.S. Open title in 1968, the first male African-American to do so. Two years later, Ashe won the Australian Open. In 1975 he became the first African-American to win the singles title at Wimbledon, beating the favorite, Jimmy Connors.

In 1969 Ashe left the amateur ranks and became a professional tennis player and, in 1972 co-founded the Association of Tennis Professionals (ATP).

After a heart attack ended his tennis career, he became more involved in activism, protesting against apartheid in South Africa and establishing tennis programs for underprivileged children.

After heart surgery in1983 he contracted the AIDS virus from a tainted blood supply. From then on until his death on February 6, 1993 he helped raise money and awareness of the disease.

In 1997 the tennis stadium in Forest Hills, N. Y. was named in his honor.

Asa Philip Randolph

Randolph was born in Crescent City, Florida April 15, 1889. The family moved to Jacksonville, Florida a few years later.

He and his brother, James, were excellent students at the Cookman Institute and Asa was good in public speaking, drama and he sang in the school's choir.

He moved to New York City to try his hand at acting but gave it up when his parents disapproved.

During WWI he and Chandler Owen, a friend he met in college, founded *"The Messenger,"* a political magazine. They championed more blacks in the military and higher wages. He ran for a couple of public offices in the 1920's as a member of the Socialist Party.

In 1925 some Pullman porters, those people, primarily black, who served the meals and waited on train passengers, asked Randolph to become head of the Brotherhood of Sleeping Car Porters. He agreed and signed up enough members to be recognized as the exclusive bargaining agent for the organization.

When President Franklin D. Roosevelt refused to end the discrimination against blacks within the defense industry, Randolph began planning a mass march on the nation's capital. Seeing this, FDR capitulated and banned discrimination throughout the industry. At Randolph's urging, President Truman eventually desegregated the military six years later.

Dr. Martin Luther King named Randolph chairman of the March on Washington in 1963. President Lyndon Johnson honored him with the Medal of Freedom.

In poor health, he retired from the Porters Union and wrote his autobiography. He died May 16, 1979 in New York City at age 90.

Benjamin O. Davis, Jr.

At age 13, one of the pilots at a barn-storming exhibition offered Davis a ride. It was the start of his career as a fighter pilot.

Born December 18, 1912 in Washington, D.C. he secured a spot at the Military Academy at West Point, New York where, along with his studies he endured and overcame intense racial discrimination.

He graduated 35th in his class of 278. When he became a second lieutenant in the infantry, he became one of only two black combat officers in the Army, the other being his father, Benjamin Davis, Sr.

Like his father before him he was assigned to teach a military tactics course at the Tuskegee Institute where he was eventually promoted to Lieutenant Colonel.

In spite of the prestige as a teacher, Davis wanted to fly. Pressure was mounting on President Franklin D. Roosevelt to have more blacks in the military. The administration created an all-black squadron and in July 1942, Davis became commander of the 99th Pursuit Squadron, the Tuskegee Airmen.

The squadron succeeded despite jealousy and racial discrimination and put to rest any further doubts, when in January 1944 the Tuskegee Airmen shot down a dozen German fighter planes in a two-day period while protecting the Anzio beachhead.

In Italy, the squadron provided escorts for bombers as they flew missions deep in German territory.

After the war, as commander of the 13th Air Force, he was promoted to Brigadier General, the first black general in the Air Force.

Still rising in the ranks, President Bill Clinton added his fourth star on February 1, 1970.

Benjamin O. Davis, Sr.

Davis was born July 1, 1877 in Washington, D.C.

He enlisted as a private in the army in July 1899 and was sent to the Philippines where he eventually rose to the rank of Sergeant-Major.

In 1901 Davis passed the tests and was commissioned a second lieutenant in the Tenth Cavalry.

Because of racial prejudice his promotions came slowly and in 1937 he was appointed commander of the 369th Cavalry, New York National Guard.

In 1939 he was able to persuade Chief of Staff George C. Marshall to convert his regiment from a support unit to anti-aircraft duty, showing Marshall African-Americans were as capable as white soldiers.

During his years in the military he spent a lot of time teaching others military science and tactics as a professor at Wilberforce University in Ohio and the Tuskegee Institute in Alabama.

He held many posts during World War II including assistant to the Inspector General.

He was especially valuable as an adviser on African-American issues in Europe.

President Franklin D. Roosevelt had Davis promoted to Brigadier General making him the first African-American general in the army. He was assigned to help about 100,000 blacks enter the Army.

He also paved the way for other African-Americans to become officers including his own son who became the first black general in the Air Force.

Benjamin Mays

Mays was born in the town of Ninety-Six, South Carolina August 1, 1894 or 1895 to tenant farmer parents who were former slaves.

His mother valued education and took his place in the fields so Benjamin could go to school.

In 1920 he graduated from Bates College in Maine and then went to the University of Chicago where he earned a Ph.D. in religion in 1935.

His education in Chicago was interrupted several times as he accepted teaching positions at Morehouse College in Atlanta and at South Carolina State College.

In 1936 Mays traveled to India where he met Mahatma Gandhi. After speaking with Gandhi, who favored a non-violent solution to problems, Mays was convinced Gandhi's principles might be stronger than brute force. It became the identifying theme of the civil rights movement.

Mays became president of Morehouse College in 1940 where he met and mentored Martin Luther King, one of his students. The two became lasting friends.

He was an excellent administrator at Morehouse and a successful fundraiser who led the college to national prominence.

During his lifetime, Mays wrote articles for newspapers and longer, thought-provoking studies which were well received.

Even after his retirement from Morehouse in 1967, he remained active in social and political circles working to improve the lives of all. He died in Atlanta March 28, 1984.

Bernard Lafayette

Lafayette was born in Tampa, Florida July 19, 1940.

He moved to Nashville, Tennessee to attend American Baptist Theological Seminary in 1958.

A strong proponent of non-violent protest he helped organize the Student Non-Violent Coordinating Committee (SNCC) in 1960.

The following year he joined the Freedom Rides that challenged segregation on interstate buses. When those buses reached Birmingham, Alabama the riders were savagely beaten by mobs. They met the same fate in Montgomery. In Jackson, Mississippi Lafayette and the others were arrested and served 40 days in prison.

Undaunted, Lafayette continued to challenge the system and was with Martin Luther King and others on the march from Selma to Montgomery in 1965.

After taking classes in non-violent protest he taught what he learned to gang leaders in Chicago and recruited them to patrol the area's slums during non-violent marches for fair housing.

When Dr. King was assassinated in 1968, Lafayette worked with the Southern Christian Leadership Conference (SCLC) to organize the Poor Peoples March on Washington, D. C. Tens of thousands of poor people and their supporters set up tents and temporary cardboard shelters showing leaders of the federal government what poverty looks like.

Lafayette has written a number of publications including a training manual for non-violent protest.

He's currently a Distinguished Senior Scholar in Residence at Emory University in Atlanta.

Billie Holiday

Billy Holiday was born April 7, 1915 in Philadelphia, Pennsylvania. She led a tough life fighting drugs and alcohol abuse most of her 44 years and was one of the most influential jazz singers of all time.

She found relief singing along to the songs of Louis Armstrong and Bessie Smith. She had no formal voice training but she began singing in clubs in the early 1930's and was eventually discovered by producer John Hammond while she was singing at a Harlem nightclub. Hammond paired her with bandleader Benny Goodman.

Goodman was a relative unknown clarinet player and leader of a band which included Jack Teagarden, Gene Krupa and Joe Sullivan. Her first recording was, "Your Mother's Son-in-Law" in November 1933.

In 1935 she made recordings with Teddy Wilson and band members from Count Basie's band which launched her career as a jazz singer.

Saxophonist Lester Young, who was part of Count Basie's orchestra, befriended Holiday and gave her the nickname, "Lady Day."

Holiday toured with the Basie orchestra in 1937. The following year she worked with Artie Shaw and his orchestra, one of the first African-American female singers to work with a white orchestra.

Some of her more popular songs include, "The Man I Love," "God Bless the Child," and "I Wished on the Moon." She told her life story in 1956 in a book entitled, "Lady Sings the Blues" which was made into a motion picture starring Diana Ross.

Her final performance was May 25, 1959 in New York City, two months before she died.

Booker T. Washington

Booker Taliaferro Washington was born into slavery on April 5, 1856. His mother worked as a cook for a plantation owner. They lived in a one room log cabin.

When the Civil War ended in 1865, he and his mother moved to Malden, West Virginia where she met and married Washington Ferguson, a free black. Booker took the first name of his stepfather as his last name.

Always interested in becoming educated, he eventually was able to attend school one hour a day thanks to Viola Ruffner for whom he worked as a houseboy.

Washington enrolled in what is now Hampton University in 1872 and worked as a janitor to pay tuition. He graduated in 1875 and was offered a teaching job at Hampton. The Alabama legislature, in 1881, approved money for a "colored" school and Washington became the head of the Tuskegee Normal and Industrial Institute. The school, which became Tuskegee University, had no equipment, two run-down buildings and very little money. Washington spent much of his time fundraising and making improvements to the campus. Under his leadership Tuskegee University became one of the leading schools in the country.

Washington's philosophy said the best interests of black people were in the trade industries and farming and the acceptance of social segregation. That stance provoked the ire of W.E.B. DeBois who championed full equality for African-Americans.

Washington did have the ear of two presidents, Theodore Roosevelt, who invited him to the White House, the first African-American so honored, and William Howard Taft. Both men used him as an advisor on racial matters.

Washington remained head of Tuskegee University until his death November 14, 1915 at the age of 59.

Carter G. Woodson

The past held Woodson's interest. Black History was his passion.

"The Father of Black History" was born in 1875 in New Canton, Virginia to former slaves.

Working in the fields made it difficult to go to school but by the time he was 17 years old he had mastered the basics. By age 20, eager for more education he worked as a miner while a student at Douglass High School where he earned his diploma.

He eventually returned to Douglass High School as its principal. He received a Bachelor of Literature from Berea College in Kentucky.

After college he worked in the Philippines as an education superintendent for the U.S. government. When he returned to America he enrolled in the University of Chicago where he received a Bachelor of Arts degree and a master's degree.

Continuing his education, he received a Ph.D. in history from Harvard University in 1912.

He devoted his life to make black history important to others and thought the best way to achieve this was to have a special time set aside for its celebration.

He said, "Those who have no record of what their forebears have accomplished lose the inspiration which comes from the teaching of biography and history."

He lobbied schools and organizations for the creation of a Black History Month. It began in 1926 as Black History Week. He picked the month of February because of the birthdays to two civil rights icons, Frederick Douglass and Abraham Lincoln.

Woodson died April 3, 1950. His legacy, Black History Month, has endured and is celebrated each year.

Charles R. Drew

Drew was born June 3, 1904 in the nation's capital, Washington, D. C., one of four children of Richard and Nora Burrell Drew.

An enterprising youngster, he became a paper boy, selling newspapers on the street corner. Soon, he had several other boys working for him covering other areas of town.

While Washington was still segregated, some of the public schools were excellent and he attended Dunbar High School where he excelled in athletics. He graduated from Dunbar in 1922 and went to Amherst College in Massachusetts on an athletic scholarship.

He had developed an interest in medical science while in high school and after graduating from Amherst, he attended McGill University Faculty of Medicine in Montreal, Canada. During his internship at Montreal General Hospital he became interested with transfusion and other fluid replacement.

He returned to the U. S. joining the faculty at Howard University College of Medicine where he trained with prominent doctors in their field. While interning at Presbyterian Hospital in New York City he also pursued a doctorate from Columbia University. He discovered that, unlike whole blood, which deteriorates after a few days, the blood plasma can be preserved for long periods of time and can be substituted for blood during transfusions. He set up an experimental blood bank at Presbyterian Hospital and wrote about it in a medical journal.

This medical breakthrough got the attention of the American Red Cross and, in 1941, they asked Drew to set up a blood bank program in the U.S.

His blood bank program saved many lives during World War II and the program became his legacy.

Charles Rangel

On June 28, 2016 Charles Rangel voted for someone other than himself for the first time in 46 years. At 86 years of age, the New York legislator retired from the U.S. House of Representatives

Rangel was born June 11, 1930 in New York City. His father was abusive and rarely worked. He left the family when Charles was six years old.

He attended DeWitt Clinton High School and was an excellent student in spite of often being truant. He dropped out of school in 1947 and enlisted in the Army a year later. He served in the Korean War earning a Purple Heart and a Bronze Star for bravery.

After his service, he earned his G.E.D and went to the New York University School of Commerce where he used the G.I. Bill to pay for school. He received his law degree from St. John's University in 1960.

He participated in a number of civil rights actions: the 1965 march from Selma to Montgomery, Alabama with Dr. Martin Luther King, Jr., and the anti-apartheid rally held in front of the South African Consulate in New York in 1984.

In 1970, after having served two terms as New York State Assemblyman, he won election to the U.S. House of Representatives, beating the incumbent, Adam Clayton Powell in the Democratic primary. One of his first actions was co-founding the CBC, the Congressional Black Caucus.

One of his goals in Congress was to have a seat on the powerful House Ways and Means Committee. That body has jurisdiction over all taxation, tariffs and other revenue-raising measures. Rangel became a member in 1974 and its chairman in 2007.

He compiled his opinions and stories in his 2007 memoir called, *"And I Haven't Had a Bad Day Since: From the Streets of Harlem to the Halls of Congress."*

Charles Sherrod

Charles Sherrod joined SNCC, the Student Non-Violent Coordinating Committee in 1960 and took part in the first demonstrations and voter registration drives.

The oldest of seven children born to a 14 year-old mother in 1937, he had to work to help support his family.

Sherrod and Cordell Reagan opened an SNCC office close to Albany State College, an all-black school. On November 1, a month after he became the first field secretary and SNCC director in southwest Georgia, he staged his first sit-in at the bus terminal. A recently passed law had desegregated bus and train stations and Sherrod wanted to test the law. The demonstration was blocked by law enforcement personnel, a violation of the statute. For the next two years Sherrod led protests, attended by thousands of students who joined the demonstrations.

His specialty was recruiting and developing local leadership. He also welcomed white workers to help with voter registration and other issues. He wanted to show blacks and whites as equals.

Sherrod left SNCC when Stokely Carmichael became chairman and expelled all white members from the organization.

In 1967 he received his Doctor of Divinity degree from the Union Theological Seminary in New York City. Returning to Albany he created the Southwest Georgia Independent Voters Project for Community Education.

In 1976 he was elected to the Albany City Council and served until 1990. In 1996, he ran unsuccessfully for Georgia State Senate.

He currently lives in Albany, Georgia.

Cheney, Goodman and Schwerner

During the Civil Rights Movement of the 1960's, many Americans of all faiths and ethnicities protested the discrimination against African-Americans, primarily in the south.

James Cheney, a 21-year old African-American was born in Meridian, Mississippi and joined CORE, the Congress of Racial Equality. He was part of a movement to register Black voters in the south.

He took part in the Freedom Rides challenging racial segregation on buses and in bus terminals.

Andrew Goodman was born in New York City November 23, 1943 and, while still in high school, participated in a March for Integrated Schools. As a member of CORE, he travelled south to help Blacks in Mississippi register to vote and to protest racial discrimination. He met Cheney and Goodman in Ohio while in training for the mission.

Michael Schwerner attended the Walden School after spending his youth in New York City. He left Columbia University to take a job as a social worker at a housing project in Manhattan. He also became involved in the Civil Rights Movement and joined CORE. He and his wife, Rita, moved to Meridian, Mississippi to work in the CORE office there. His activism was noticed by segregationists and members of the Ku Klux Klan.

On June 21, 1964 the three were found murdered near Philadelphia, Mississippi. Although 18 men were arrested, none were charged with the crime.

Forty-one years later, 80-year-old Edgar Ray Killen, was charged with three counts of murder and sentenced to 60 years in prison

Colin Powell

Powell was born April 5, 1937 in Harlem, New York.

He didn't know what career he wanted when he graduated from Morris High School but when he entered the Reserve Officer Training Corps (ROTC) at the City College of New York he had found his calling.

Sent to South Vietnam in 1963 he was wounded by a booby-trap which earned him the Purple Heart medal.

After the war he enrolled at George Washington University in Washington, D. C. earning an MBA.

After a tour of duty in Korea he entered the National War College. He was promoted to brigadier general in 1976 and commanded a brigade of the 101st Airborne Division.

Powell joined the Jimmy Carter administration as assistant to the deputy secretary of defense where he received his second star. He held a number of positions in the federal government. In 1987 he became National Security Advisor to President Ronald Reagan.

In 1989, Powell, now a four-star general, became Chairman of the Joint Chiefs of Staff, the first African-American to hold the post.

He retired from the Army in 1993 and two years later wrote his autobiography, *My American Journey."*

In 2000, President George W. Bush appointed Powell the first African-American secretary of state and he served until 2004.

Powell, now retired, continues to be aware of national and international events and comments on them from time to time. His leadership over the years has been an inspiration to many.

Condoleezza Rice

This future Secretary of State was born in Birmingham, Alabama November 14, 1954.

Although born in the deep south where racial segregation was an everyday occurrence, her parents sought to give her every advantage.

An accomplished pianist she also took French and Spanish lessons in school and was a competitive figure skater. An extremely good student, she skipped first grade and was promoted from the sixth grade to the eighth. She received a Bachelor of Arts degree in political science from the University of Denver, her master's degree from Notre Dame and her doctorate from the Graduate School of International Studies at the University of Denver.

Rice taught political science at Stanford University. In 1987 she was an advisor to the Joint Chiefs of Staff and two years later became director of Soviet and East European Affairs on the National Security Council.

After serving briefly in the White House she returned to Stanford and, from 1993 to 1999 was the school's first female provost. She had taken classes in Russian language and history and had become an authority on foreign policy.

In 2001 she succeeded Colin Powell as National Security Advisor in the George W. Bush administration helping shape American foreign policy. Her job became more difficult on September 11, 2001 when terrorists flew commercial airplanes into the World Trade Center and the Pentagon.

On November 16, 2004 she was nominated for Secretary of State by President Bush and assumed to post two months later.

In spite of her accomplishments, she says, perhaps jokingly, she would love to become commissioner of the National Football League.

Coretta Scott King

King was born near Marion, Alabama on April 27, 1927 to parents who valued a good education. King went to Lincoln High School, a private school in Marion. She then won a partial scholarship to Antioch College where she studied music and voice.

While in college she joined a number of organizations devoted to civil rights including the NAACP.

In 1951 she attended Boston's New England Conservatory of Music where she was introduced to a Baptist Minister, Martin Luther King. They were married June 18, 1953.

With Martin, she travelled the world meeting leaders and the common people advocating for the rights of minorities and women.

Back home she participated in the marches and sit-ins and boycotts that would eventually see success in the Civil Rights Act of 1964 and the Voting Rights Act of 1965.

After the assassination of her husband in 1968, she founded the Martin Luther King Jr. Center for Nonviolent Social Change, known as the King Center, in Atlanta.

Shortly after the assassination, Coretta Scott King led a march that was planned before Martin's death, on behalf of the sanitation workers in Memphis, Tennessee. In May 1968 she helped start the "Poor People's Campaign," an effort to gain economic justice for poor people in the country.

For years she lobbied for a national day of recognition for her husband. Martin Luther King Jr. day was finally approved and is celebrated on January 15th each year.

Coretta Scott King died in her sleep January 30, 2006.

Diane Nash

Nash was born May 15, 1938 in Chicago, Illinois where she attended parochial and public schools.

She attended Howard University in Washington, D.C. before transferring to Fisk University in Nashville where she experienced racial segregation for the first time.

Unsure of whether non-violent protest was effective she was amazed at the risks people took staging sit-ins and other types of protests which eventually changed her mind. She joined the sit-ins at local Nashville department stores and lunch counters. Their efforts were successful as Nashville became the first southern city to desegregate lunch counters.

In April 1960, Nash and others founded SNCC, the Student Non-Violent Coordinating Committee in Raleigh, N.C.

A year later she helped coordinate the Freedom Rides across the Deep South and served as liaison between the press and the U.S. Department of Justice.

She eventually dropped out of college to work for the SCLC, the Southern Christian Leadership Conference and Dr. Martin Luther King, Jr.

In 1961 she married James Bevel, a fellow activist and civil rights leader. They moved to Jackson, Mississippi where she registered voters and worked for school desegregation for the SCLC.

After the passage of the Civil Rights Act of 1964 and the Voting Rights Act of 1965, Nash turned her attention to the Vietnam Peace Movement.

She continues to remain involved in political and social issues.

Dick Gregory

Born October 12, 1932 in St. Louis, Missouri, Gregory was raised by his mother after his father disappeared for good.

He was a track star at Sumner High School and continued running track at Southern Illinois University. He was drafted into the Army in 1954 attached to Special Services where he was able to develop his talent for comedy.

His big break came in 1961 when he filled in at the Playboy club in Chicago for another comedian. He faced an audience of white southern businessmen and had them laughing at his jokes and stories.

During his comedy routines he satirized racism and used the day's headlines and current events to comment on social issues. He agreed to appear on *"The Jack Paar Show"*, the forerunner of *"The Tonight Show"* only after Paar agreed to interview him after his performance. Before that, black performers did their routines, and then left the stage.

Using his fame, he became active in the Civil Rights Movement speaking at voter registration drives, performing benefit shows for civil rights organizations, joining the march from Selma to Montgomery and protesting segregation and discrimination.

While trying to be a peacekeeper during the riots in the Watts section of Los Angeles in 1965, he was shot in the leg. His activism cost him. Club owners were reluctant to hire him because they never knew when he might leave to join a march or to protest an injustice.

In 1967 he ran unsuccessfully against Richard Daley for mayor of Chicago and a year later ran for president of the United States on the Peace and Freedom Party ticket. As a write-in candidate he received more than 47,000 votes.

Richard Claxton Gregory died August 19, 2017 at age 84.

Dorie Miller

Doris Miller was born October 12, 1919 in Waco, Texas.

As a young man he worked on his father's farm. At Moore High School he played football and was very athletic.

In 1938 he enlisted in the Navy to help support his parents. Because the military was segregated, combat jobs weren't available to African-Americans so Miller became a cook.

On January 2, 1940 he was assigned to the *USS West Virginia*, nicknamed the "Wee Vee." It was berthed at Pearl Harbor, Hawaii. On December 7, 1941 Miller was preparing breakfast when the Japanese attacked just after 8 a.m.

Miller ran to his battle station, an anti-aircraft gun, only to find it had been hit by torpedoes and was useless. He was ordered to evacuate the wounded including his captain who later died of his wounds.

Seeing an unattended 50 caliber Browning anti-aircraft gun Miller began firing at Japanese planes even though he had no training on the gun he was firing. After the planes left the scene, he continued rescuing the wounded and those struggling in the water. The *"West Virginia"* eventually sank.

When news of Miller's heroism reached his superiors, he was awarded the Navy Cross, second only to the Medal of Honor. Miller became the first African-American honored with the Navy Cross.

Miller was then assigned to the USS Liscome Bay which saw action in the Pacific. At 5:10 a.m., November 24, 1943, the ship was torpedoed near the bomb magazine, which detonated. A year and a day later Miller was presumed dead, one of 646 who died that day in 1943.

Dorothy Height

Height was born in Richmond, Virginia March 24, 1912. She attended integrated schools when her family moved to Rankin, Pennsylvania.

She was a good speaker in high school and became politically active championing civil rights causes and women's issues.

After being rejected by Barnard College in New York she attended New York University where she earned a Bachelor of Education Degree and a Master's Degree in psychology.

While working at the Harlem YWCA in 1937 she met Mary McLeod Bethune and first lady Eleanor Roosevelt when they visited the facility. Bethune was president of the National Council of Negro Women and before they left the "Y" Height had volunteered to help. Twenty years later Height became president of the organization.

In 1946, Height was directing the integration of all the YWCA's. In 1965 she created the Center for Racial Justice. Because of her involvement in these organizations she became a leading figure in the civil rights movement working with major national leaders like Whitney Young, James Farmer and Martin Luther King.

In 1963 she and others organized the March on Washington where King gave his "I have a dream" speech.

Turning her sights to women's issues, she helped found the National Women's Political Caucus in 1971 along with Gloria Steinem, Betty Friedan and Shirley Chisholm.

Dorothy Height died on April 20, 2010 in the nation's capital.

The United States Postal Service honored her with a postage stamp issued February 1, 2017.

Dorothy Johnson Vaughan

Vaughnn entered this world on September 20, 1910 in Kansas City, Missouri.

She graduated high school with a full college scholarship to Wilberforce University in Ohio. She graduated there at age 19 with a B. A. degree in French and one in mathematics.

To help her parents during the Great Depression, she taught math at a high school in Virginia.

At 22, she married Howard Vaughan and they moved to Newport News, Virginia.

She applied for a job she thought was temporary at the National Advisory Committee for Aeronautics which, in 1958, became the National Aeronautics and Space Administration (NASA).

She was assigned to a segregated unit in the computer room with other African-American women working on experiments for the space program.

When the group's supervisor died, Vaughan was appointed her replacement, becoming the first black woman promoted at NASA. The promotion gave her wide latitude and she was able to converse with other computer technicians and supervisors, mostly white, who provided her with valuable information.

She became an authority on the computer language, FORTRAN, and taught it to others.

Vaughan remained at NASA for 28 years working in a variety of jobs until her retirement in 1971.

Dorothy Vaughan died November 10, 2008 at the age of 98.

Duke Ellington

Edward Kennedy Ellington was born April 29, 1899 in Washington, D. C.

He became interested in music as a young man and soon found himself a member of a jazz band which played in small venues in the nation's capital.

In 1923 the band, Ellington among them, moved to New York City and got a gig in Times Square at the Hollywood Club. Four years later they moved to the famed Cotton Club in Harlem.

Ellington and the band gained a following due to radio broadcasts from the club. He also took the band to Broadway to play in musicals. In 1930 the band went to California to appear in a movie and one of Ellington's compositions, "Three Little Words," was used in the film. It hit number one on the pop charts.

In 1933 the band toured Europe to rave reviews. Meanwhile Ellington continued to write music, the lyrics of which were written at a later date. Among them were "Sophisticated Lady," "In a Sentimental Mood," "Prelude to a Kiss" and the classic, "Satin Doll."

After WWII the Big Band sound grew less popular but Ellington kept composing and the band continued to play his classics. He was able to keep the band together using his royalties from his songwriting. Duke was also able to provide the score for some movies and he also wrote longer pieces.

The Newport Jazz Festival revitalized the genre and Ellington's music. He and the band continued to tour successfully until his death.

Ellington was a visionary who was a composer and bandleader who set the tone for the evolution of American jazz. His many musical compositions became standards. He died May 24, 1974 in New York.

Edward W. Brooke III

Edward Brooke was a man of many firsts: the first African-American elected to the U.S. Senate by popular vote; the first African-American elected Attorney General in any state and the first Black to be nominated for statewide office in Massachusetts. Even though he was a pioneer in breaking barriers, he never liked the idea of being associated with the phrase, "first something."

Brooke was born October 26, 1919 in the nation's capital, Washington, D.C. His father was a lawyer and he had a middle-class upbringing.

He attended Howard University and earned a bachelor's degree in sociology. He was also a reservist during college and in 1941, after the Japanese attack on Hawaii, he was commissioned a second lieutenant and joined the 366th Combat Infantry Regiment, an all-Black unit. After black troops were permitted to serve in combat, it had previously been restricted to white troops, Brooke rose to the rank of captain and earned the Bronze Star and the Combat Infantryman Badge.

After leaving the military he enrolled in Boston University's School of Law where he became an editor of the Law Review. He eventually returned to Boston University to earn his master's degree in law.

In 1947 he married Remigia Ferrari-Scacco, a woman he met during the war.

Brooke, a life-long Republican, began his political career in 1950 when he ran for state representative. He lost that race and the one in 1952. In 1960 he lost his race for secretary of state. Two years later, however, he won the office of attorney general of Massachusetts. In 1966 he was successful in securing a seat in the U.S. Senate.

In 2002, he was diagnosed with breast cancer. A double mastectomy rendered him cancer free.

Ella Baker

Baker was born in Norfolk, Virginia December 13, 1903 the grand-daughter of slaves.

For most of her life she worked behind the scenes of the civil rights movement.

She attended Shaw University, graduating in 1927 as valedictorian of her class.

She moved to Harlem, New York and joined a number of civil rights organizations including the NAACP which sent her to the south to organize chapters there.

In 1957 she helped organize the Southern Christian Leadership Conference (SCLC) and found a young man to run it: Reverend Dr. Martin Luther King, Jr.

Three years later she heard of a sit-in at a Woolworth's store in Greensboro, North Carolina. Wanting to include young people as activists in the movement she created SNCC, the Student Non-Violent Coordinating Committee.

In 1961 SNCC and CORE, the Congress of Racial Equality, organized the Freedom Riders, volunteers who rode buses to the deep south to register black voters.

In 1964 she helped organize a new political party, The Mississippi Freedom Democratic Party, to challenge the views of the national Democratic Party and change their focus to voting irregularities in the south.

Her behind the scenes activism were an essential part of the civil rights movement. She died on her birthday in 1986 in New York City.

Emmett Till

Emmett Till grew up on the south side of Chicago and went to a segregated elementary school. His mother, Mamie, always warned him to be careful around other people, but it didn't stop Emmett from playing pranks.

In August 1955, Till's great-uncle, Moses Wright came to Chicago to visit. When Wright was ready to return to Mississippi Emmett begged to go with him. Reluctantly, Mamie gave in.

Three days after arriving in Money, Mississippi the 14-year-old joined a group of teenagers and went to Bryan's Grocery and Meat Market to buy refreshments. Emmett bought some chewing gum.

Theories abound as to what happened inside the store. One account has Till whistling at a white woman in the store. Another says, on a dare, he asked the white cashier for a date, another says he walked past the white woman and said, "Bye Baby." Still others have him flirting or touching the hand of the owner's wife, Carolyn Bryant.

When Roy Bryant returned from a business trip four days later and was told about the incident with his wife, he and his half-brother, J. W. Milam kidnapped Emmett from his great-uncle's home. They brutally beat him, shot him in the head and threw his body in the Tallahatchie River. When the body was recovered it was unrecognizable. Emmett was identified by a ring he was wearing.

Roy Bryant and J. W. Milam went on trial in a segregated courthouse and were found not guilty. Emmett's body was returned to Chicago where his mother demanded an open casket so everyone could see the brutality against her son.

In a 2007 interview, Carolyn Bryant Donham admitted she had lied about Till's behavior 52 years earlier.

Ethel Waters

Waters was born October 31,1896 in Chester, Pennsylvania, the daughter of a teenaged rape victim.

She grew up poor living in the slums of Philadelphia and never staying in the same place for more than a few weeks or months.

At 17, persuaded by friends, she sang a few songs at her birthday party, held at a nightclub, and wowed her audience. At the party were two vaudeville producers who signed her to a contract.

In1919 she moved to New York City and sang in the nightclubs of Harlem. She kept touring the country with her vaudeville troupe and continued to perform in primarily black clubs.

A friend, Earl Dancer, convinced her to perform before white audiences where she became a huge star earning more than she did at black venues.

Hollywood found she was as talented on the screen as she was in nightclubs. Her first movie was *"On with the Show"* in 1929. In 1949 she received an Academy Award nomination for the film *"Pinky."* She was nominated again in 1953 for *"Member of the Wedding."*

In 1939, having read the book, she starred on the stage as Hagar in "Mamba's Daughter," a story that mimicked her childhood.

A deeply religious woman, in the 1950's she joined the Billy Graham Crusade and toured the country. Still performing in films and doing an occasional guest appearance on television or at clubs she was devoted to Graham and his message. She remained with the Billy Graham Campaign until her death September 1, 1977.

Eubie Blake

James Hubert Blake was born to freed slaves on February 7, 1883 in Baltimore, Maryland.

He began playing the pump organ at four or five years old and when he was in his teens, he played piano in brothels and bars.

During one of those performances, in 1899, he played an original tune he composed called, "The Charleston Rag."

Around the turn of the century he was playing in night clubs and touring, eventually moving to the Goldfield Hotel in Baltimore where his reputation grew as a performer and entertainer.

In 1910 Blake and Avis Lee were married. She was a classical pianist.

In 1915 he teamed up with Noble Sissle, a singer and lyricist and together they wrote songs.

After World War 1 the two went into Vaudeville. They were able to team with Flournoy Miller and Aubrey Lyles to produce an all-black Broadway show. Opening on May 23, 1921, "Shuffle Along" was performed more than 500 times on the Great White Way. One of the songs in the play, "I'm just wild about Harry," went on to become a classic. "Shuffle Along" became another contribution to the Harlem Renaissance of the 1920's.

Blake and Sissle continued to write music for other shows including "Memories of You," featured in the show "Blackbirds of 1930."

With the revival of ragtime music in the 1950's Blake became popular again. He was still performing and entertaining at 98 years old.

He died on February 12, 1983.

Eugene Bullard

Bullard was born in Columbus, Ga. in 1895.

He ran away from home when he was 11 years old and travelled with a band of Gypsies throughout Georgia.

The group talked of how blacks were better treated in Europe than in America so in 1912 Bullard stowed away on a German merchant ship and landed in Aberdeen, Scotland.

To earn a living, he became a prize fighter. Moving to Paris he continued boxing and became a promoter of boxing matches.

When France entered World War One, he joined the French Foreign Legion and participated in a number of battles including Verdun, where he was wounded. He also received the Croix de Guerre for his bravery in battle.

Unable to return to the infantry, he was offered a position with the French Flying Corps making him the first black fighter pilot. He flew 20 missions and shot down two enemy planes.

When the U.S. entered the war in 1917, he applied to the U.S. Air Force. His application was never processed.

As World War Two approached he joined the French resistance. He opened a nightclub where occupying German troops congregated. Bullard, who spoke fluent German, was able to learn valuable information. He was smuggled out of France to avoid being captured and interrogated by the Gestapo.

He lived in New York working as an elevator operator at Rockefeller Center. When he died in 1961, he was buried with full French military honors in the French section of a N.Y. cemetery.

Fanny Lou Hamer

Hamer began working in the fields only six years after she was born on October 6, 1917 in Montgomery County, Mississippi.

She dropped out of school at age 12 to help her sharecropper family pick cotton. When the farm owner learned she could read and write he had her do all the record-keeping.

In 1945 she married Perry "Pap" Hamer who operated the tractor on the farm. She couldn't have children of her own because when she went to the hospital to have a tumor removed, doctors also performed a hysterectomy without her consent. She eventually adopted two boys and two girls from poor families.

At age 37 she saw a sign posted by the Student Non-Violent Coordinating Committee (SNCC) and investigated. She joined and became a field worker on the voter registration committee which taught blacks to read and write so they could register to vote. Hamer passed the voter registration test on her third try.

In June 1963, while coming home from a voter registration workshop, she was arrested with others on the bus when they tried to order food at a restaurant in Mississippi. She was severely beaten while in jail sustaining kidney damage, a blood clot in her eye and a limp.

She ran unsuccessfully for Congress in the Mississippi Democratic Primary in 1964 but continued to speak out against injustice.

In 1972, the Mississippi House of Representatives passed a resolution praising her contribution to civil rights.

She died March 21, 1977 of breast cancer.

Frank Robinson

Robinson was born August, 31, 1935 in Beaumont, Texas.

He played baseball in high school and when he graduated, he signed with the Cincinnati Reds baseball team of the National League.

In 1956 he was named Rookie of the Year and then named Most Valuable Player in 1961.

His batting style had him crowding home plate which often resulted in his getting hit by pitched balls. He was also an aggressive runner bowling over defenders guarding the bases.

Just before the 1966 season began Robinson was traded to the American League's Baltimore Orioles. That year he won the Triple Crown of baseball with a .316 batting average, 49 home runs and 122 runs batted in. He was unanimously voted the American League's Most Valuable Player becoming the only player to win MVP in both leagues.

On May 8, 1966 Robinson tagged a pitched ball and sent it flying completely out of Memorial Stadium, a home run measured 541 feet.

Robinson, however, had bigger plans than just being a player. He wanted to manage a major league team.

In 1975, the Cleveland Indians made him a player/manager making him the first black manager in the major leagues. In his first at-bat with the Indians, he homered off "Doc" Medich of the Yankees.

He then joined the Giants and became the first black manager in the National League.

Robinson was inducted into the Baseball Hall of Fame in 1982.

Fred Shuttlesworth

Shuttlesworth, whose given name was Freddie Lee Robinson, was born on March 18, 1922 in Mount Meigs, Alabama. He took the last name of his stepfather.

He studied religion and the ministry, earning his B.A. degree in 1951 from Selma University and a B.S. degree from Alabama State College.

In 1957 he joined Martin Luther King and others to found the Southern Christian Leadership Conference (SCLC) which became the premiere organization fighting racial discrimination.

When the state of Alabama outlawed the NAACP, Shuttlesworth created the Alabama Christian Movement for Human Rights, continuing its work.

While still advocating non-violence, Shuttlesworth was more aggressive than Dr. King, more "in your face" confrontational. He persuaded King to make Birmingham the focus of the Civil Rights Movement. He organized demonstrations, marches and protests by children and young people. He constantly challenged "Bull" Connor, Birmingham's public safety commissioner. He was one of the organizers of the Selma to Montgomery March in 1965.

He had moved to Cincinnati, Ohio in 1965 to become pastor of a black church, but made frequent trips to the south.

On March 7, 2007 Shuttlesworth returned to Selma joining presidential candidates Barack Obama and Hillary Clinton and hundreds of supporters including some who were at the original march in 1965 as they recreated the crossing of the Edmund Pettus Bridge.

That year he moved back to Birmingham where he died October 5, 2011 at age 89.

Frederick Douglass

Douglass was born in 1818. No one is sure of the exact date but later in life he chose February 14.

He was born a slave and as a toddler was taken from his mother as was the custom.

At age 12 he was sent to his master's relatives in Baltimore, Maryland. It was there he learned the alphabet and how to read by watching and listening to others read. When sent to other plantations he taught slaves there how to read the New Testament.

After several attempts, Douglass escaped with the help of Anna Murray, a free slave, whom he later married. They settled in New Bedford, Massachusetts. In 1839 he became a licensed preacher.

Douglass began speaking out against slavery and joined a group giving speeches throughout the country. He also wrote three books about his life. With the income from his books he was able to travel to Ireland and Great Britain where he continued to lecture. He returned to America in 1847.

A year after returning from Europe he attended the first women's rights convention at which Elizabeth Cady Stanton demanded that women be given the right to vote. Douglass spoke in favor of it.

He was a proponent of the civil war seeing it as a vehicle with which to end slavery. He recruited black troops and became an advisor to President Lincoln.

Douglass moved to the nation's capital to become U.S. Marshal for the District of Columbia. He continued to travel and speak out.

He received a vote for president at the 1888 Republican National Convention. He died of heart failure February 20, 1895.

George Washington Carver

Carver was born into slavery around 1861 near Diamond Grove, Missouri.

Shortly after George's birth he was kidnapped with his mother and sister and were sold in Kentucky. Their owner, Moses Carver rescued George but couldn't help the others.

When the Civil War ended, Moses Carver and his wife kept George and had him educated at home.

Leaving the Carver plantation as a young boy he travelled to a school for black children 10 miles away. After attending different schools, he received his diploma from Minneapolis High School in Minneapolis, Kansas.

He enrolled in the botany program at Iowa State then returned to Alabama after graduation to direct the Department of Agriculture at the Tuskegee Institute.

He devoted his time to research. He explored methods of soil management, crop rotation and alternative crops to replace cotton. He recommended planting peanuts and soybeans to revitalize the soil with nitrogen. To increase the use of these alternative crops he developed marketing tools to educate people finding dozens of uses for these plants.

His fame grew and prominent people sought his advice including President Theodore Roosevelt and Mahatma Gandhi.

Carver lived a simple life never seeking monetary rewards and staying out of the political arena.

Carver died January 5, 1943 after falling down stairs in his home. He was 78 years old.

Gladys West

Gladys West was born in 1930 in Sutherland, Virginia. Her parents had a small farm and West wanted nothing to do with it.

Studying hard she graduated at the top of her class which guaranteed her a full scholarship which she used to attend Virginia State University.

She was encouraged to study either science or math. She selected math and after graduation became a teacher in Sussex County for two years. Returning to school she was awarded her master's degree and went to work at the Naval Surface Warfare Center, Dahlgren Division.

She took on the challenging job of defining the shape of the Earth as it relates to sea level. During her years at the Warfare Center she wrote manuals, technical specifications and worked with computers to find the ideal altitude for satellites in space. Her work eventually led to the creation of the Global Positioning System (GPS) which today is used to find and direct humans to every part of the Earth, it's accuracy to within miles or feet.

She also worked as project manager for the Seasat radar altimetry project which tested various oceanographic sensors to gain a better understanding of the Earth's seas.

While Pluto is no longer designated a planet, West took part in a study that proved the regularity of that planet's motion relative to its neighbor, Neptune.

She worked at the Dahlgren Division for 42 years, retiring in 1998.

On December 6, 2018, she was inducted into the Air Force Space and Missile Pioneers Hall of Fame during a ceremony at the Pentagon.

Granville Woods

Called the "Black Edison," Woods invented many improvements in the railroad industry.

Woods was born April 23, 1856 in Columbus, Ohio to free blacks.

He didn't have much of a formal education but he learned while working at a number of jobs including blacksmith and machinist.

Knowing the importance of education, he studied electronics and engineering during his spare time.

He held many different jobs within the railroad industry and because of that he began thinking of ways to improve safety and communications.

Many cities today still have overhead electrical wires used to provide power to trains and trolleys. Woods developed that system in 1888.

Communications between the train engineer and stations along the route was poor. An engineer in one train didn't know where other trains were located on the same track so collisions were frequent. Woods patented the Synchronous Multiplex Railway Telegraph which provided communications between stations and moving trains. Now every engineer knew where every other train was located which prevented derailments and injuries.

Woods was sued by Thomas Edison when Edison claimed patent infringement. After Woods won the suit Edison offered him a partnership which Woods turned down.

Woods continued inventing, creating the automatic air brake, a steam boiler furnace and a grooved metal wheel for trolleys.

Woods died January 30, 1910.

Gwendolyn Brooks

Brooks was born June 7, 1917 in Topeka, Kansas and grew up in Chicago, Illinois.

Because she was shy, she turned to writing to pass the time and that writing became poetry.

"Eventide", one of her early poems was published in *"American Childhood,"* when she was 13 years old. She became a frequent contributor of poetry to the *"Chicago Defender,"* a predominantly black newspaper.

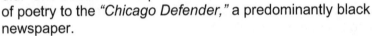
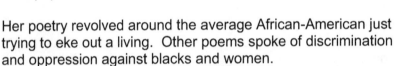

Her poetry revolved around the average African-American just trying to eke out a living. Other poems spoke of discrimination and oppression against blacks and women.

In 1945 she published her first book of poetry, "A Street in Bronzeville," which was highly acclaimed and projected her as a serious poet, one to be reckoned with.

Her second book of poems, "Annie Allen," won "Poetry" magazine's Eunice Tietjens prize in 1949. A year later she won the coveted Pulitzer Prize for poetry for "Annie Allen", the first African-American to be so honored. She was also selected poet laureate of Illinois.

She wrote one novel, "Maud Martha," depicting prejudice from light-skinned blacks as well as white people, things she experienced as a young woman. It was her only novel.

In later books she became more political and complex in her poetry. She also penned her biography.

She died of cancer December 3, 2000 in Chicago.

Harriet Beecher Stowe

Stowe was born June 14, 1811 in Litchfield Connecticut, the seventh child of Reverend Lyman and Roxanna Foote Beecher.

The family moved to Cincinnati, Ohio in 1832 and while Harriet wasn't exposed to slavery, it was prevalent in Kentucky just across the border. She eventually saw how the slaves were treated and it affected her greatly.

In 1836 she married Calvin Stowe, the brother of a close friend, Eliza Stowe who had taken ill and died. She and Calvin moved to Maine in 1850 where she wrote *"Uncle Tom's Cabin,"* the story of a slave and his cruel master.

The book sold more than 300,000 copies in the first year and was a huge success. Northerners learned of the harsh life of the slaves in the south while Southerners considered it propaganda. Nevertheless, it got people talking about the issue. It was originally serialized each week in *"The National Era"* newspaper. It eventually was put in book form in 1852.

Because of the book, many people learned of the horrors of slavery and became abolitionists, people who wanted to abolish it.

The book also became an international phenomenon educating people on slavery, the southern plantation and the slave owner.

Stowe did research before writing the book. She met with slaves and used their stories to dramatize her narrative.

President Abraham Lincoln, jokingly, said Harriet Beecher Stowe's book was one of the reasons for the start of the "War Between the States."

Stowe died July 1, 1896 at the age of 85 in Hartford, Connecticut.

Harriet Tubman

She was the fifth of nine children of Harriet and Benjamin Ross, born into slavery in 1822 on the Maryland plantation of Anthony Thompson.

As a young teen she was almost killed while working in the fields when she was struck in the head by an iron weight thrown by an overseer at another fleeing slave.

She married John Tubman, a free black man around 1844. With the death of the plantation owner she fled to Philadelphia using the Underground Railroad in the fall of 1849. She left behind her husband and her family.

From 1850 to 1860 she organized more than a dozen escapes which included her husband, her parents, family members and more than 70 others. She returned to the south more than 19 times to lead slaves to freedom.

A reward for her capture, reaching as high as $40,000, didn't deter her from risking her life and freedom to secure a better life for others.

During the Civil War she provided nursing care to black soldiers and newly liberated slaves. She also served as a scout and spy for the Union Army.

When the war ended, she returned to Auburn, New York becoming a community activist, humanitarian and suffragist. Tubman also turned her home into a place of refuge for indigent and aging blacks.

Money was always a problem in the upkeep of the home and other necessities so she financed her endeavors by selling copies of her biography and giving speeches.

Harriet Ross Tubman died March 10, 1913 in Auburn, New York at the age of 91.

Harry S. Truman

Truman was born May 8, 1884 in Lamar, Missouri and lived his early years in Independence, Missouri.

His ancestors had owned slaves and he grew up in a racist city. The racism and discrimination of others reflected his own views of blacks, Chinese and Jews.

Truman joined the Missouri National Guard which was called to action at the onset of World War I and his unit was sent to France. By the end of the war Truman's personal views changed when he witnessed the murder and assaults on his fellow black soldiers.

From 1919 to 1922 he ran a clothing store in Kansas City and in 1934 was elected to the U.S. Senate having served a number of years as a county judge. He was known for his fairness and honesty.

In 1944 he was nominated to be Franklin Delano Roosevelt's vice-presidential running mate primarily because he was seen as a moderate from the Midwest.

When Roosevelt died in 1945, Truman became president. One of his acts was to establish a committee on civil rights, tasked with finding solutions to discrimination. Congress ignored the findings of the committee so Truman, by executive order, desegregated the military requiring all members of the armed forces be treated equally.

No one gave him a chance to win the election of 1948 but his energy and persistence paid off as he made whistle-stops by train around the country. The Chicago Tribune prematurely published an edition declaring New York Governor Thomas Dewey the winner.

When Truman left the presidency, he returned to Independence to write his memoir and walk as a regular citizen. He died December 26, 1972. He's buried, with his wife Bess, at the Truman Library.

Harvey Gantt

Gantt was born January 14, 1943 in Charleston, South Carolina.

He became active in the civil rights movement while still in high school.

Gantt was a student at Iowa State University and then applied to Clemson University in South Carolina. Clemson denied black students' admission, so Gantt sued the school. The U.S. Court of Appeals sided with Gantt and he became the first African-American student at the school.

He graduated Clemson with honors and a degree in architecture then received his Master's degree at the Massachusetts Institute of Technology (MIT).

In 1971 he opened an architectural firm in Charlotte, North Carolina with Jeffrey Huberman.

His political career began in 1974 when he was appointed to the Charlotte City Council. He served until 1983 when he was elected mayor. He served two terms, the first black mayor of the Queen City.

He twice ran for the U.S. Senate against incumbent Jesse Helms but narrowly lost both races.

He has continued his public service having served on the North Carolina Democratic Party Executive Council, the Democratic National Committee and the National Capital Planning Commission in Washington, D.C.

He still manages his architectural firm in Charlotte.

Hattie McDaniel

She was born June 10, 1895 in Wichita, Kansas. Her father was a man of many talents: minister, entertainer, banjo player and carpenter.

He moved his family to Denver, Colorado in 1901 and Hattie was enrolled in a school in which she was one of only two black students in her class.

She started performing in minstrel shows and in 1909 joined her brother's show after dropping out of school.

She moved to Los Angeles, California where her brother, Sam, was a regular on a radio program. He got Hattie a job as a performer where she became a favorite of listeners.

In 1934 she was given a role in the movie, *"Judas Priest"* where she sang a duet with humorist Will Rogers. Playing a servant in another movie some African-American journalists accused her of stereotyping slaves as happy being enslaved rather than being free.

As a serious Hollywood actress, jobs started coming her way. Most of them were roles where she portrayed servants or maids to a white household.

She won the role for which she is famous, Mammy, in "Gone with the Wind," over many others seeking the part. Her salary was $450 a week. The film was a hit in its 1939 showing and McDaniel won an Oscar for Best Performance by an Actress at the Academy Awards ceremony in 1940, becoming the first African-American to win an Oscar. Ironically, all black actors, McDaniel included, were barred from attending the film's debut because of racial discrimination.

Hattie McDaniel died October 26, 1952 in Los Angeles. She was awarded two stars on Hollywood's Walk of Fame and her likeness appeared on a U.S. postage stamp in 2006.

Hiram Rhodes Revels

Revels was born September 27, 1827 in Fayetteville, North Carolina to parents who weren't slaves.

He was educated at a local school prior to attending the Beech Grove Quaker Seminary in Liberty, Indiana.

He was ordained a minister in the African Methodist Episcopal Church. Eventually, accepting a pastorate in St. Louis, Missouri. Leaving the Midwest, he moved to Baltimore, Maryland working with his brother Willie at a Presbyterian church.

During the civil war he helped recruit some all-black regiments from Maryland, then returned to St. Louis to open a school for blacks. After serving in churches in Kentucky and Louisiana he finally settled in Natchez, Mississippi.

Because of his leadership in educating blacks he was noticed by the Republican Party. His first elected position was as an alderman. He later won a seat in the state legislature, one of 30 blacks serving there.

When Mississippi seceded from the Union two U.S. senators resigned their seats in that chamber. They remained vacant until 1870. The Mississippi legislature, wanting to fill those seats, at least one with a black candidate, chose Revels for one of them.

Upon arriving in Washington to be sworn in, the Democrats refused to seat him claiming Revels wasn't a citizen for the nine-year requirement and his citizenship only began when the 14th amendment was passed, in 1868, After considerable debate, Revels was sworn in as a senator, becoming the first black man elected to Congress.

When his term ended a year later, he returned to Mississippi to become president of Alcorn University.

Isaiah DeQuincey Newman

I. Dequincey Newman has the distinction of being the first African-American to be elected to the South Carolina Senate since reconstruction.

Born April 17, 1911 he was an enterprising youngster who earned money shining shoes on street corners.

He attended Williamsburg County public schools and then attended Claflin College in Orangeburg. His bachelor of arts degree came from Clark College in Atlanta. Following his father in the ministry he earned his divinity degree from Gammon Theological Seminary in Atlanta.

Newman helped organize the Orangeburg branch of the NAACP in 1943 and served as field director for South Carolina for nine years during the height of the Civil Rights Movement.

His quiet and dignified manner and his adherence to non-violent protest and negotiation helped him gain the respect of the white leadership.

Feeling the Republican Party no longer represented African-Americans he joined the Democrats and became a confidant to the state's political leadership and a delegate to many Democratic national conventions.

As a minister he worked to improve conditions for blacks and whites in rural South Carolina. He chaired the Governor's Council on Rural Development.

On October 25, 1983 he won election to the S. C. Senate and was warmly welcomed by his peers.

Because of ill health he resigned from the Senate on July 31, 1985 and died three months later.

Ida B. Wells

Wells was born July 16, 1862 in Holly Springs, Mississippi.

She was educated at Shaw University, a school started by her father, James.

In 1878 she lost her parents and a brother to yellow fever. Rather than seeing her family split apart, she got a job as a teacher to care for her remaining brothers and sisters.

She got her brothers jobs as carpentry apprentices, a job her father held, then moved to Memphis with the girls. While waiting for a teaching job she accepted employment in Woodstock, a suburb of Memphis.

While on the train from Memphis to Woodstock she refused a conductor's demand to leave the first-class section, for which she had a ticket, to the smoker car, where blacks usually sat. She was forcibly removed from the train. She sued the railroad and won, only to be overruled by the Tennessee Supreme Court.

She started writing about injustices in church newspapers and when she had saved enough, became part owner of the "Free Speech and Headlight" newspaper in Memphis.

After three friends were lynched, she moved to New York City joining the staff of the "New York Age."

She lectured in Europe for a while then returned to the U.S. settling in Chicago where she married attorney Ferdinand Lee Barnett in 1895.

Continuing to fight for minority rights she joined W. E. B. DuBose and others in creating the NAACP IN 1909.

She died March 5 1931 in Chicago.

Jackie Robinson

Robinson was born January 31, 1919 in Cairo, Georgia, the youngest of five children.

He played a variety of sports at Pasadena Junior College in California where he spent his youth.

He joined the Army in 1942 and a year later was commissioned a second lieutenant.

Upon his discharge he played baseball in Hawaii and with the Kansas City Monarchs of the Negro Leagues.

Branch Rickey, president of the National League's Brooklyn Dodgers was looking for a player to integrate professional baseball which, at the time, had no black players.

Rickey bought Robinson's contract and sent him to the all-white Montreal Royals, suspecting his ball player would be subjected to some intense racial provocation. Rickey received assurance from Robinson that he would not respond to the taunts and racial slurs from players and fans.

Robinson excelled in the minor leagues with a .349 batting average and a .985 fielding average, good enough to be brought up to the major leagues, becoming the first black player in major league baseball. His first game for the Dodgers was on April 15, 1947. He led the National League in stolen bases and was named Rookie of the Year.

At away games he still suffered the taunts and slurs of fans and opposing players. They lessened considerably when Dodger shortstop Pee Wee Reese openly showed his acceptance of his second base teammate.

After retiring from baseball in 1957 he became an activist in the civil rights movement becoming a spokesman for the NAACP and other organizations.

James Baldwin

Baldwin was born in Harlem, New York August 2, 1924. His father was a preacher and at age 14 he became one too.

When he graduated from Dewitt Clinton High School, he knew he wanted to be a writer.

Earning a fellowship helped him travel to Europe where he didn't have to worry about segregation and he could devote all his time to his writing. He wrote three books while there.

When he returned to America, he became a spokesman for the civil rights movement. He wrote essays which were published in the leading magazines and newspapers at the time decrying the violence in the south.

Baldwin also wrote plays in the turbulent 1960's which were produced on Broadway. One of them, *"Blues for Mr. Charley"* was based on the murder of Emmett Till.

Because of his writings and his activism, he became one of the most important and influential writers of the 20th century.

His books, essays and plays told stories of the life of the black community, the importance of the church and the distrust toward the police.

The deaths of Martin Luther King, Malcolm X and Medgar Edgars affected him greatly. So much that he returned to France in the 1970's to escape the homophobia and racism in America.

He kept his American citizenship even though he spent most of the final 15 years of his life in Europe.

He died November 30, 1987 in Saint-Paul-de-Vance, France of stomach cancer and was buried in Harlem.

James E. Clyburn

Clyburn was born July 21, 1940 in Sumter, South Carolina.

He became interested in politics when a hospital in Charleston, S.C. went on strike. Helping settle the dispute, he worked on the campaign of St. Julian Devine who was elected to the city council of Charleston in 1969.

After an unsuccessful run for the S. C. General Assembly he joined the staff of Governor John C. West as an advisor, becoming the first black advisor to a S. C. sitting governor.

After the Orangeburg Massacre (noted elsewhere in this book) Governor West appointed Clyburn head of the Human Affairs Commission. He held that post until his run for a seat at the U.S. House of Representatives. He won, in a gerrymandered district, in 1992 and has been re-elected since.

He's held a number of important positions in the House: Vice-chairman of the Democratic Caucus in 2003; chairman of the caucus in 2006; majority whip (2007 & 2018) and chairman of the Congressional Black Caucus.

He has championed a number of issues during his tenure including healthcare (increasing community health centers), education (providing more money for special education and lower interest rates on federal student loans), Charleston's ports, (deepening the ports to allow larger cargo ships access); labor issues (increasing the minimum wage) and the environment (opposed to any off-shore drilling and promoting nuclear energy).

He met his wife, Emily, in jail during the civil rights movement and they married in 1961. They have three grown daughters.

James Meredith

His attempts to register as a student at the University of Mississippi were repeatedly denied but that didn't stop James Meredith.

Born June 25, 1933 in Kosciusko. Mississippi, he served in the Air Force before attending Jackson State University.

In 1961 he applied for admission to the University of Mississippi. After he was denied he filed a racial discrimination lawsuit which made its way through the lower courts to the U.S. Supreme Court.

Mississippi state officials ignored the Supreme Court ruling and continued barring Meredith and other black applicants from enrolling.

Fearing violence, U.S. Attorney General Robert F. Kennedy called out federal troops to protect Meredith and allow him to register for classes.

He graduated in 1963 and earned a law degree from Columbia University in 1968.

He returned to the south organizing the "Walk against fear," a march from Memphis, Tennessee to Jackson, Mississippi to oppose the violence against African-Americans for exercising their right to vote. As he crossed into Mississippi he was shot and wounded by an unknown assailant. While he was hospitalized the march was continued by Roy Wilkins, Whitney Young, Martin Luther King and other civil rights leaders. Meredith rejoined the march the day before they reached the state capital.

His career has included a run for a congressional seat in Mississippi.

He's an author and lecturer today.

Jesse Jackson

Jackson was born out of wedlock October 8, 1941 in Greenville, South Carolina. A few months after he was born, his mother, Helen Burns, married Charles Henry Jackson who adopted the boy.

He played baseball, basketball and football in high school and was class president. He attended the University of Illinois before transferring to North Carolina A&T.

While there he became active in the civil rights movement protesting discrimination and segregation. He was one of the "Greenville 8," who protested the all-white public library with a sit-in.

He then attended the Chicago Theological Seminary and when Dr. Martin Luther King began his march from Selma to Montgomery, Alabama, Jackson was there with other divinity students taking on leadership roles where needed.

In 1971 he organized People United to Serve Humanity, "Operation Push." In 1984 he created the Rainbow Coalition to lobby for equal rights for all Americans and to demand more social programs and voting rights for minorities. His work with PUSH and other organizations brought him notoriety which he used to run, unsuccessfully, for president of the United States in 1984 and 1988.

Because of his world-wide stature, Jackson was able to negotiate the release of hostages and political prisoners held in foreign countries.

In 1990 a new position was created to lobby Congress to make Washington, D. C. a separate state. Jackson was chosen to lead it.

In 1996 "Operation Push" and the Rainbow Coalition merged to form the Rainbow Push Coalition with headquarters in Chicago.

Jesse Owens

Born September 12, 1913, Jesse
Owens was a track star in high
school and at Ohio State University.

He set records in the 100-yard and
200-yard dashes as well as the long
jump while still at East Technical
High School in Cleveland, Ohio.

He succeeded in spite of several
bouts of chronic bronchial congestion
and pneumonia. He was even
expected to work in the fields picking
cotton.

At a tournament in 1935 he set three records and tied another.
He won four events at the NCAA championships that year
including three at the Olympic trials.

The 1936 Olympics were held in Berlin, Germany and Adolph
Hitler wanted to use the games to showcase what he considered
to be his superior athletes. Those white competitors were
supposed to be the best in the world and he berated America for
having black athletes on their team.

The United States won 11 gold medals at the games, six of them
won by black athletes. Owens alone won four gold medals and
broke two Olympic records. He became the star of the games and
a national sensation.

He returned home, not to a hero's welcome, but to the same
segregated America he had left. In 1976 President Gerald Ford
gave Owens the recognition he deserved by presenting him the
Presidential Medal of Freedom.

Owens died of lung cancer on March 31, 1980. Ten years later he
was posthumously awarded the Congressional Gold Medal.

John Lewis

The son of sharecroppers, John Lewis was born February 21, 1940 near Troy, Alabama.

Inspired by the words and actions of civil rights activists he decided to take a more active role in the civil rights movement.

He took part in the Nashville sit-ins while a student at Fisk University. Those actions were responsible for the desegregation of lunch counters in the city.

In 1961 he took part in the Freedom Rides, challenging racial discrimination in the south. During one of those rides he was severely beaten by mobs and arrested by law enforcement personnel.

By 1963 he was chairman of the Student Non-Violent Coordinating Committee (SNCC) and helped organize the March on Washington where Dr. Martin Luther King would give his "I Have a Dream" speech.

When Andrew Young resigned his congressional seat in January 1977 to become U.S. Ambassador to the United Nations, Lewis ran for Congress and lost to Atlanta City Councilman, Wyche Fowler. In 1981 he ran successfully for a seat on the Atlanta City Council.

When Fowler won election to the Senate after nine years in the U.S. House of Representatives, Lewis ran for his seat and was elected to Congress in 1986.

He's been honored many times by national and international institutions and was the recipient of the Medal of Freedom, America's highest civilian honor.

One magazine called him the "Conscience of the Congress" where he serves with distinction today.

Joseph Lowery

Joseph Lowery, known as the "Dean of the Civil Rights Movement," was born October 6, 1921 (or 1924) in Huntsville, Alabama.

Growing up in the segregated south, he felt the sting of racial discrimination first hand. At the age of 12, he was beaten by a white police officer for accidentally bumping into the law enforcement official.

After high school he went to a number of colleges and received his bachelor's degree from Paine College in Augusta, Georgia. Looking to serve in the ministry he graduated from the Chicago Ecumenical Institute in 1950 with a Doctor of Divinity degree.

Two years later he began serving as pastor at the Warren Street United Methodist Church in Mobile, Alabama. He helped end discrimination on Mobile's bus system using some of the same tactics which ended segregation on buses in Montgomery, Alabama.

Working with Dr. Martin Luther King, Ralph David Abernathy and others he helped create the Southern Christian Leadership Conference and he became its vice president. In 1977 he was named president.

In 1964, Lowery moved to Birmingham, Alabama to become pastor of St. Paul's Church. He continued to be involved in protests and demonstrations including the 1965 march from Selma to Montgomery, Alabama.

After Birmingham, he pastored at Central Church and Cascade United Methodist Church in Atlanta.

Lowery retired from the ministry in 1992 but has remained active in the community.

Josephine Baker

Freda Josephine MacDonald was born in a black neighborhood in St. Louis, Missouri on June 3, 1906.

Her father hired her out at eight years old as a maid and by age 14 she had left home and left behind a husband.

To survive she became a street dancer and eventually joined an African-American theater group. Taking her second husband's last name and her middle name Josephine Baker thrived as a dancer in many Vaudeville shows.

She moved to New York City and took part in the Harlem Renaissance, the celebration of black life and art.

Learning there was more money to be made in Europe she went to Paris, France and became a star on the continent through her dancing, singing and unique costumes. She even appeared in several motion pictures.

When the Nazi's invaded France she became a spy, listening to the conversations of German military personnel and relaying it to the allies, the information written in invisible ink on sheet music.

In August 1963 she returned to the United States to find a country segregated by race and rife with discrimination. She attended Martin Luther King Jr.'s March on Washington that year where she spoke about her life in America and abroad. She continued to fight for equal justice throughout the early 1970's.

She never had children of her own so she adopted 12 children from different countries and took them on the road with her.

In declining health, she had two heart attacks and a stroke, she returned to Paris in 1975 to star in a 50th anniversary review honoring her first arrival in the French capital. It was a huge success. Four days later, April 12, 1975 she died of a stroke.

Julian Bond

As one of the founding members of SNCC, the Student Non-Violent Coordinating Committee, and as chairman of the NAACP, Bond had, for years, been an activist for civil and human rights.

He was born January 14, 1940 in Nashville, Tennessee.

As a student at Morehouse College he founded an organization whose protests won the integration of Atlanta's movie theaters, lunch counters and parks.

He served four terms in the Georgia House of Representatives and six terms in the state Senate. He sponsored or co-sponsored more than 60 bills which became law including a landmark sickle-cell testing program.

He was president of the Southern Poverty Law Center, an organization he co-founded, from 1971 to 1979. He also served as president of the Atlanta chapter of the NAACP before becoming chairman of the national organization.

In 1968 he was nominated for vice president of the United States, the first African-American so honored. He had to decline because, at the time, he was too young to be eligible for the office.

He continued his activism as president-emeritus of the Southern Poverty Law Center and as a founding member of the Atlanta Black-Jewish Coalition. He was a commentator for NBC, a newspaper columnist and a poet.

At the University of Virginia, he was a professor of history and he served as an adjunct professor at American University.

Bond died August 15, 2015. Representative John Lewis said of him, "He was so smart, so gifted, so articulate and he had a way of getting to people, to students, to young people and he succeeded."

Julius Rosenwald

Rosenwald was born August 12, 1832 to German Jewish immigrant parents. He was raised a few blocks from the home of Abraham Lincoln in Springfield, Illinois.

He became apprenticed in his teens to his uncles in New York City to learn the clothing trade. Later, with his brother Morris, he started a clothing manufacturing company which went bankrupt in the recession of 1885.

With help from his cousin, Julius Weil, the Rosenwald brothers founded Rosenwald and Weil Clothiers in Chicago. In 1893, Richard Sears and Alvah Roebuck changed their company name to Sears, Roebuck and Company and stocked the clothes made by Rosenwald and Weil.

Roebuck sold his half of the company to Sears who sold Roebuck's shares to Julius Rosenwald and his brother-in-law. Rosenwald diversified the merchandise to include dry goods, hardware, furniture and other products. When Sears retired, Rosenwald was named president of the company. In 1924 Rosenwald resigned the presidency to devote more time to philanthropy.

Some years earlier, Rosenwald had met Booker T. Washington who asked Julius to serve on the board of the Tuskegee Institute. He provided financial support to relieve Washington from fundraising challenges so he could devote more time running the institute.

At Washington's urging, Rosenwald provided funds to build six small schools in rural Alabama for African-American students. He would eventually build more than 5,000 schools, called "Rosenwald Schools" in the South.

He also planned the development of more than 400 apartment units in Chicago for African-Americans to counter segregation in housing.

Katherine Johnson

Born in White Sulphur Springs, West Virginia, August 26, 1918, Johnson was to become a leading figure in America's space program.

She graduated West Virginia State College summa cum laude at age 18 with degrees in mathematics and French.

She went on to teach math and French at various schools in Virginia and West Virginia.

Learning that the National Advisory Committee for Aeronautics was hiring mathematicians she applied for a job and began working at the Langley Research Center in Hampton, Virginia.

A natural curiosity and inquisitive mind got her promoted to Langley's flight research division.

In 1958, NACA became NASA, the National Aeronautics and Space Administration and Johnson and others were tasked with calculating how to get a man into space and bring him home safely. She was the one who plotted Alan Shepard's flight plan, the astronaut who would become the first American in space.

She then worked on the second phase, sending a manned spacecraft into orbit around the Earth. John Glenn, the astronaut who first orbited this planet, refused to fly that mission unless the computer's results were verified by Katherine Johnson.

Johnson continued her career at NASA working on the Apollo 11 mission to the moon and prospective Mars missions.

President Barack Obama awarded her the Medal of Freedom, America's highest honor for civilians in 2015.

Langston Hughes

Langston Hughes was born in Joplin, Missouri February 1, 1902.

He began writing poetry in his early teens, poetry highly regarded by his teachers and peers. After graduating from high school, he wrote *"The Negro Speaks of Rivers"* which was published in *"The Crisis"* in 1921.

He attended Columbia University in New York City and while there toured Harlem becoming enamored with that part of the city.

He continued writing poetry, winning an *"Opportunity"* magazine award in 1925. He was introduced to Alfred Knopf whose company published a collection of his poems known as *"The Weary Blues."*

Hughes was part of what is called the Harlem Renaissance, the development of the area into a black cultural entity thriving with stage performances, art, literature and music.

Hughes travelled extensively around the world and in the Deep South and continued to write poetry and prose. He was also a newspaper correspondent during the Spanish Civil War.

In 1935 his play, *"Mulatto,"* premiered on Broadway, one of many plays he would write. At age 28 he wrote his first autobiography, *"The Big Sea."*

Hughes documented black life, their African roots and culture, as he put those words into poems, short stories, operas and stage plays and longer prose.

He was known as the "Poet Laureate of the Negro Race."

Hughes died May 22, 1967 after abdominal surgery.

Larry Doby

He played football, basketball and baseball and earned a scholarship to Long Island University, but Larry Doby will forever be remembered as the man who broke the color barrier in baseball's American League.

Doby was born December 12, 1923 in Camden, South Carolina.

He played baseball at Mather Academy in Camden. Richard DuBose taught him how to play the game.

Doby graduated from high school in 1938 and moved to Patterson, New Jersey where his mother had moved earlier. At Eastside High School he earned 11 varsity letters in baseball, basketball, football and track. He also played semi-pro ball in the Negro Leagues with the Newark Eagles.

He spent three years in the navy and rejoined the Eagles in 1947. He wasn't going to stay with the team very long. Bill Veeck, owner of the Cleveland Indians was looking to integrate his team. He bought Doby's contract from the Eagles and put him in the starting lineup July 5, 1947 when the Indians were playing Chicago.

Doby endured segregated hotels and death threats to become a Hall of Fame outfielder with the Indians. He was an All-Star for seven of his 13 years in the major leagues.

He also played for the Chicago White Sox and the Detroit Tigers and was a coach for the Montreal Expos.

In 1978 Bill Veeck made him manager of the White Sox, making him the second African-American major league manager.

He was elected to Baseball's Hall of Fame in 1998. He died June 17, 2003 after a long illness.

Leontyne Price

Leontyne's mother, Kate Baker Price, sang in the church choir and she encouraged her daughter when she showed an interest in music.

Mary Violet Lyontyne Price was born February 10, 1927 in Laurel, Mississippi. She was an outstanding pianist and sang in the glee club at her high school.

She was originally studying music education but was encouraged to concentrate more on voice. After graduation she was offered a full scholarship to the Juilliard School of Music in New York City where she was the featured soprano in many of the school's productions.

Virgil Thompson saw one of her performances and invited her to star in a revival of his opera, *"Four Saints in Three Acts."* Two months later she would appear in the role that would define her – Bess in George Gershwin's opera, *"Porgy and Bess."* During the opera's tour she married Porgy, her co-star, William Warfield.

During the 1950's she performed in many operatic productions in the United States and abroad and in many different venues. In February 1955 she made her television debut in Puccini's *"Tosca."* A year later starred in the NBC production of Mozart's *"The Magic Flute."*

On July 2, 1958 she played at Covent Garden in London, her European debut, and then on to La Scala in Milan, Italy, the most prominent opera house in Europe, where she sang the title role in *"Aida."* She became the first black singer at this venerable music hall.

After singing the role of Leonora in *"Il Trovatore,"* her debut at the Metropolitan Opera House in New York City in 1961, she became one of the principal sopranos at the "Met."

She gave her farewell performance on January 3, 1985 at the "Met" reprising her role in *"Aida."*

Levi Coffin

Born October 28, 1798 Coffin became known as the President of the Underground Railroad.

Coffin grew up on a farm and didn't have a formal education, however, he did open a school for slaves in New Garden, North Carolina.

Even though he lived in the south he was opposed to slavery.

When he moved to Newport, Indiana he found he was on the route of the Underground Railroad which helped slaves escape to the north. He made his home a depot where slaves could spend some time resting before they continued their journey north.

While many of his neighbors refused to house slaves, they did provide food and clothing for them. During their time in Indiana Coffin and his wife Catherine helped thousands of slaves reach safety.

It is said the Coffins were the inspiration for Harriet Beecher Stowe's novel, *"Uncle Tom's Cabin."*

In 1847 Coffin and his wife moved to Cincinnati, Ohio where he opened a wholesale store selling merchandise made by freed slaves.

When the Civil War began, he joined the Freedmen and worked to help liberated slaves.

In 1864 he travelled to England and organized a Freedmen's Aid Society there. The organization sent money and supplies to America to help with the cause.

During the last years of his life Coffin wrote his autobiography, *"Reminiscences of Levi Coffin."* He died September 16, 1877.

Lillian Wald

Born to a German-Jewish family in Cincinnati, Ohio Lillian Wald would become one of the founders of the NAACP.

In 1878, when she was 11 years old, her family moved to Rochester, New York where she attended Miss Cruttenden's English-French Boarding and Day School for Young Ladies.

In 1889 she was a student at New York Hospital's School of Nursing where she graduated two years later. She also took classes at the Woman's Medical College. She left medical school and began a class on nursing for poor immigrant families in New York's Lower East Side. She moved into the neighborhood to better serve her patients.

Wald was the founder of the Henry Street Settlement, secretly funded by Philanthropist Jacob Schiff, whose mission was to help poor Russian Jews who immigrated to America. Her nursing staff grew and donations increased that by 1913 her staff was 92 strong and the Settlement had become the Visiting Nurse Service of New York.

She was a community organizer who was involved in the labor movement improving working conditions for women and lobbying the federal government to provide educational benefits for children while banning child labor laws.

Wald was a strong advocate of civil rights and insisted that all Henry Street classes be racially integrated. In 1909 she became a founding member of the NAACP. The organization's first major public conference was held at the Henry Street Settlement.

The "New York Times" named her one of the 12 living American women in 1922. Never married, Wald died of a cerebral hemorrhage on September 1, 1940. Over 2,000 people gathered at Carnegie Hall for a tribute to her a few months after her passing.

Louis Armstrong

Armstrong was born August 4, 1901 in New Orleans, Louisiana.

After he shot a gun in the air when he was 12, he was sent to a home for boys where he met Peter Davis. Davis taught him how to play the cornet.

Another cornet player, Joe "King" Oliver liked what he heard and took Armstrong with him to Chicago where Louis joined Oliver's Creole Jazz Band.

While he enjoyed playing in Oliver's band his wife encouraged him to go out on his own. Taking her advice, he played with a number of bands recording records with them. He started recording under his own name and with his newly formed bands, the Hot Fives and the Hot Sevens. In 1926 he switched from the cornet to the trumpet. By 1932 everyone knew him by his nickname, *"Satchmo."*

His popularity grew and he found work in films and on radio while continuing his recording sessions. In 1935 he met and hired Joe Glaser as his manager.

When the era of the big bands began to fade, Armstrong fronted a smaller band with top named talent like Jack Teagarden, Earl Hines and other jazz greats.

In addition to playing an instrument, Armstrong began to sing, in a raspy voice, sometimes interspersing scat singing throughout the song.

He recorded a number of songs that became hits including "Blueberry Hill," "Mack the Knife," "Hello Dolly" and "What a Wonderful World." His rendition of "Hello Dolly" knocked The Beatles off the top spot on the pop charts in1964 making him the oldest musician to have a number one hit in *Billboard Magazine's* history.

Years of touring took a toll on his body and doctors told him to rest. He kept practicing though and died July 6, 1971 of a heart attack.

Lyndon Baines Johnson

Johnson, born August 27, 1908, saw the effects of poverty growing up in Stonewall, Texas. To help pay for his tuition at Southwest Texas State Teacher's College, today, Texas State University, he taught students of Mexican descent.

In 1937, upon the death of the incumbent member of the U.S. House of Representatives, he scored a surprise victory to fill the seat.

After a short tour in the Navy during World War II, he was elected to the Senate in 1948, where, five years later he became the youngest Minority Leader in Senate history. When the Democrats took control of the upper house a year later, he became Majority Leader.

When President Kennedy was assassinated on November 22, 1963, Johnson became the 36th president and he used his persuasive ability to pass legislation Kennedy championed including the civil rights act of 1964 which outlawed segregation and discrimination throughout the country.

Shortly after, he outlined his vision for a "Great Society," with emphasis on health and education, urban problems, housing and transportation, civil rights and the beautification of America. Between 1965 and 1968, more than 200 pieces of legislation was passed including the Voting Rights Act of 1965 which made discrimination in voting illegal and paved the way for millions of African-Americans to register and vote. He also appointed Thurgood Marshall to the U.S. Supreme Court, the first African-American to serve on the high court.

Much of his time, however, was devoted to the war in Vietnam. In 1968, seeing the country divided over the issue, with no solution in sight, Johnson stunned the nation by not running for re-election.

He died suddenly of a heart attack on January 22, 1973.

Madam C. J. Walker

Born Sarah Breedlove on December 23,1867 near Delta, Louisiana she became a very successful businesswoman.

Her parents died by the time she was seven years old. At age 14 she married Moses McWilliams just to get away from an abusive brother-in-law. Six years later she was a widow with a daughter so she moved to St. Louis, Missouri where her brothers were barbers.

She developed a scalp condition and none of the products available provided relief so she started experimenting with her own recipes.

She married Charles Joseph Walker in 1906 and used his name from then on to sell her products. Her husband provided marketing and advertising advice, having been a newspaper advertising salesman.

She travelled the south and southeast going door-to-door selling her products. She opened a beauty college in Pittsburgh, Pennsylvania to train others in hair care. She created a work force of thousands of women who worked on commission and sold her products.

Moving to Indianapolis, Indiana in 1910, she built a factory and laboratory for continued research. She travelled to Central America and other places promoting her hair care products and searching for other ingredients useful for her company.

In 1916 she moved to Harlem, New York where she became involved in the area and worked with the NAACP in their campaign to stop lynching.

She was a philanthropist, giving money to black churches, national causes and educational organizations.

She died May 25, 1919 at the age of 51.

Mae Jemison

October 17, 1956 is the date of Mae Jemison's birth.

In 1959 her family moved from Decatur, Alabama to Chicago because the schools were better in Illinois.

She was an avid reader of anything related to space, astronomy or space travel.

She was very active in extracurricular activities at school including dance and theater productions. She graduated from Stanford University with a Bachelor of Science degree in chemical engineering. She then entered Cornell University Medical College graduating in 1981 as a medical doctor.

Putting her education and skills to work she was the Peace Corps medical officer for Sierra Leone and Liberia in Africa for 30 months.

When she returned to the U.S. in 1985, she acted on her dream of space and astronomy. In October of that year she applied for a spot in the NASA astronaut program. She was one of 15 selected to train.

On September 12, 1992 she was designated science mission specialist aboard the space shuttle "Endeavor," STS-47 Skylab-J, a cooperative mission with Japan which lasted eight days. She was co-investigator on the bone-cell research experiment flown on the mission. She also became the first African-American woman in space.

Jemison left NASA in March 1993 and began teaching at Dartmouth College. She also started her own company which encourages the love of science in young people.

She's a member of several organizations and serves as an adviser to many others.

Malcolm X

Malcolm Little was born May 19, 1925 in Omaha, Nebraska to Louise Little, a home-maker, and Rev. Earl Little, a supporter of Black Nationalist leader Marcus Garvey.

His father's civil rights activism forced them to move twice due to death threats. In 1929, their home was firebombed and two years later, Earl's body was found on the town's trolley tracks.

In 1946 Malcolm and his friend "Shorty" Jarvis were arrested and convicted of burglary. Malcolm Little was sentenced to 10 years in jail but was granted parole after seven.

During his time in prison he converted to Islam and joined the religious group, the Nation of Islam led by Elijah Muhammad. He also changed his last name to "X" saying Little was a slave name and "X" signified his lost tribe name.

Muhammad appointed Malcolm national spokesman for the Nation of Islam with the job of opening new mosques in major cities. He used all the media to spread the word increasing membership from 500 to 30,000. He soon became more famous than his mentor, Muhammad.

Malcolm and Muhammad parted ways after he learned of Elijah's infidelities. The FBI learned Malcolm was targeted for assassination.

In 1964 Malcolm travelled to Mecca where he shared his ideas with different cultures. Returning to the U.S., he founded the Organization of Afro-American Unity which held that racism, not the white race, was the greatest enemy of blacks.

On February 14, 1965 his home was firebombed. No one was injured but a week later three gunmen rushed the stage where he was speaking and shot him 15 times at close range.

Marcus Garvey

Born on the island of Jamaica August 17, 1887, Garvey became an advocate of the "Back to Africa" movement.

At age 14, he became apprenticed to a printer and eventually created the *"Negro World" newspaper.* In 1910 he travelled to Central America and wrote about the problems facing migrant workers.

Returning to Jamaica in 1912, he founded the Universal Negro Improvement Association with the goal to unite all Negros in a country governed by themselves. He came to the United States in 1916 to promote his ideas, settling in New York City.

He organized a chapter of the U.N.I.A. in New York. He also started a shipping company which would establish trade between Africans in America, the Caribbean, Central and South America, Canada and Africa. At the same time, he also created a manufacturing company.

His Negro Improvement Association had grown to over four million people by 1920 and he held a national convention in New York at Madison Square Garden which attracted more than 25,000 followers.

His successes and influence attracted not only supporters but those who thought him a threat. Even some leaders of the black community collided with his ideas and ideals. Another detractor was FBI Director, J. Edgar Hoover who had Garvey indicted for mail fraud. He was convicted in 1923, imprisoned two years and deported to Jamaica in 1927.

Undaunted, Garvey continued his work in Jamaica then moved to London, England in 1935.

He died in 1940 from a series of strokes.

Martin Luther King, Jr.

King was born January 15, 1929 in Atlanta, Georgia. He attended Booker T. Washington High School and was an accomplished public speaker.

A good student, he skipped the ninth and twelfth grades. He entered Morehouse College at 15. Even before he left college, he knew his calling was the ministry.

At Boston University he began his doctoral studies in theology. It was here he was introduced to Coretta Scott. They married on June 18, 1953.

When Rosa Parks was arrested for not giving up her seat on a Montgomery, Alabama bus, King led the bus boycott. It lasted for more than a year and ended with a district court ruling which put an end to racial segregation of all Montgomery public buses. It also propelled King into the national spotlight as spokesman for the civil rights movement.

In 1957 King, along with others, created the Southern Christian Leadership Conference (SCLC) to organize black churches and to conduct non-violent protests.

On August 28, 1963 more than 250,000 people joined the March on Washington to protest an end to racial segregation in public schools, to ban racial discrimination in employment and other issues. King delivered his "I have a Dream" speech in which he called for unity, brotherhood and the end of injustice.

On March 25, 1965 he led marchers from Selma to Montgomery, Alabama demanding equal rights for African-Americans.

On April 4, 1968 King was assassinated in Memphis, Tennessee. A Poor People's March on Washington, which King helped organize, was held shortly after his death.

Mary Jackson

Mary Jackson was born in Hampton, Virginia April 9, 1921.

She attended local schools but after graduation from high school she went to Hampton Institute where her studies led to a bachelor's degree in both political science and mathematics.

After a short stint as a school teacher she joined the National Advisory Committee for Aeronautics, the forerunner of the National Aeronautics and Space Administration (NASA).

Her career began as a research mathematician at the Langley Research Center in her hometown, Hampton. Continuing her education by taking additional courses she was promoted to Aerospace Engineer in 1958, becoming NASA's first black female engineer.

Her new job dealt with wind tunnels and their effect on different forms of aircraft, actual and theoretical.

During her NASA career, she worked in a number of divisions of the organization, writing 12 technical papers in the process.

She helped other black women advance in NASA by coaching them for tests and exams which would help with their promotions.

After 34 years at NASA she took a demotion to become a human resource administrator while still serving as the Federal Women's Program manager in the Office of Equal Opportunity.

She married Levi Jackson, Sr. and they had two children.

She died February 11, 2005 in Hampton, Va. To honor her an elementary school in Salt Lake City, Utah was named for her.

Mary McLeod Bethune

Bethune was born a child of slaves on July 10, 1875 in Mayesville, South Carolina.

Fate had other plans for Mary than picking cotton.

In 1898 she married Albertus Bethune. They moved to Palatka, Florida where she sold insurance while working at a Presbyterian Church. When her marriage ended in 1904, she founded the Daytona Normal and Industrial Institute, a boarding school for black girls.

In 1923 it merged with the Cookman Institute to become Bethune-Cookman College in Jacksonville.

After women gained the right to vote Bethune led voter registration drives and was instrumental in getting blacks to leave the Republican Party in favor of the Democratic Party during the depression years.

She was a friend of Eleanor Roosevelt, the president's wife, which may be why Franklin Delano Roosevelt named her director of Negro Affairs of the National Youth Administration, becoming the highest-ranking black woman in government.

In 1935 she created the National Council of Negro Women and served as its president for 14 years.

Besides President Roosevelt she worked for three other presidents: Calvin Coolidge, Herbert Hoover and Harry Truman.

In her later years she worked to ensure equal rights in hiring and education.

She died May 18, 1955 in Daytona Beach, Florida.

Matthew J. Perry, Jr.

Perry was born August 3, 1921 and was a graduate of Booker T. Washington High School in Columbia, S.C.

After being drafted into the Army he saw segregation first hand. Denied entry into a restaurant he was forced to receive his dinner at the restaurant window while Italian prisoners of war was being served inside.

He was awarded his law degree from South Carolina State College, now University, in 1951. He opened his law practice in Spartanburg, S.C. and in 1961 became Chief Counsel to the S.C. State Conference of the NAACP in Columbia.

Keenly aware of the problems facing blacks in the south he welcomed civil rights cases. He successfully litigated the integration of Clemson University and the University of South Carolina, won a case which resulted in the creation of single member districts throughout the state and overturned the conviction of thousands of civil rights protestors who were incarcerated solely because they participated in peaceful civil disobedience.

Many times, he accepted food and other non-cash items as payment for his services. There were times when he was forced to sit in the balcony of a courtroom instead of the gallery, waiting for his cases to be called to trial.

In 1976 President Gerald Ford appointed him to the U. S. Military Court of Appeals, the first African-American judge from the south. President Jimmy Carter appointed him South Carolina's first black district court judge in 1979.

In 2004, the new federal courthouse in Columbia was named in his honor.

Judge Perry died July 29, 2011.

Maya Angelou

Born Marguerite Johnson on April 4, 1928 she spent her childhood in St. Louis, Missouri and Stamps, Arkansas.

Her mother had a number of different careers so she spent most of her young life with her grandmother.

When she was eight years old and living with her mother, she was raped by her mother's boyfriend. He was convicted but then released only to be found beaten to death soon after. Thinking she was responsible for his death she stopped speaking for years except to her brother Bailey who eventually was able to help her overcome the trauma of the rape.

In 1959 she became the northern coordinator for the Southern Christian Leadership Conference (SCLC) after being asked to accept the post by Dr. Martin Luther King.

Angelou is known for her poetry. One of her most recognized poems, *"I know why the caged bird sings,"* was nominated for the National Book Award. President Bill Clinton asked her to write a poem for his inauguration.

Besides writing poetry, she has penned six memoirs and she won a Grammy for a recording of one of them.

Maya Angelou, a singer, composer, dancer, actor, civil rights worker, lecturer, journalist, kept herself busy.

She was the first black director in Hollywood. She produced, directed and starred in many stage, film and television productions. She wrote screenplays and musical scores and was twice nominated for a Tony Award for her acting.

A woman of words who used them to make life more beautiful.

Medgar Evers

Medgar Wiley Evers, activist in the fight for civil rights, was born July 2, 1925 in Decatur, Mississippi.

He was drafted into the Army when he was 18 years old and fought in France and Germany. He learned first-hand about segregation when he and five friends were denied the right to vote at gunpoint.

Attending Alcorn State College, he met and married a classmate, Myrlie Beasley in 1951. After graduation he sold insurance for the Magnolia Mutual Life Insurance Company headed by Theodore Howard who was also president of the Regional Council of Negro Leadership, a civil rights organization. Evers learned how to conduct boycotts, how to organize and leadership.

Denied entry into the University of Mississippi Law School, then a segregated school, he became the rallying point in the NAACP's campaign to desegregate the school. He also became the first field officer for the NAACP in Mississippi.

He moved to Jackson, Mississippi where he took part in boycotts against white merchants. He also assisted in the desegregation of the University of Mississippi.

As a prominent civil rights figure in Mississippi he constantly fought for justice and criticized the state and local legal system and its bias against people of color. He also called for a new investigation into the death of teenager, Emmett Till.

Because of his activism he became a target for hate groups and other racist organizations. His house was firebombed in May 1963 and on June 12 of that year Evers was shot in the back in his driveway. He's buried in Arlington National Cemetery.

Thirty years later his killer was finally convicted of the murder.

Modjeska Monteith Simkins

Simkins was born in Columbia, South Carolina December 5, 1899. She and her family lived on a small farm. Her mother and she sold surplus fruits and vegetables to supplement their income.

She was educated at Benedict College in Columbia and when she received her teaching degree began teaching math at Booker T. Washington School.

She married Andrew Simkins in 1929 and was forced to leave the teaching profession because the school system refused to employ married women.

She found work at the S.C. Tuberculosis Association as director of the Negro Program which informed citizens about tuberculosis and other health problems. She became more involved with the NAACP which cost her the job at the TB Association.

While a member of the NAACP she fought against inequality and for equal pay for women.

She also became involved in *Briggs v. Elliot,* a lawsuit demanding the end of segregation in schools in Clarendon County, S. C. That lawsuit and others were merged into one becoming *Brown v. Board of Education.* That lawsuit, brought before the U.S. Supreme Court, challenged the "separate but equal" provision of existing law.

She remained active in the community through charities and civil rights organizations.

In 1990 Governor Carroll Campbell Jr. awarded Simkins the "Order of the Palmetto," the highest civilian honor in South Carolina recognizing her almost 60 years of service to the state.

Simkins died April 9, 1992 and is buried in Columbia's Palmetto Cemetery.

Muhammad Ali

He was born Cassius Clay January 17, 1942 in Louisville, Kentucky

When his bicycle was stolen, he sought revenge but a Louisville police officer redirected his energy toward the boxing ring.

His first fight as an amateur was in 1954 against Ronnie O'Keefe which he won by a split decision. He also won the 1960 Olympic Gold Medal in boxing.

His first professional bout was October 29, 1960 when he won a decision after six rounds with Tunney Hunsaker. Often, before each bout he would predict the round in which he'd knock out his opponent. He was sassy, brash, confident and never afraid to speak his mind.

He fought a number of classic battles against strong and determined opponents: Olympic boxing champions, Joe Frazier (1964), Floyd Patterson (1952) and George Forman (1968). Each of them became heavyweight champions.

After his match against Heavyweight Champion Sonny Liston in which he scored a technical knockout, Cassius Clay joined the Nation of Islam and on February 27,1964, he changed his name to Muhammad Ali.

In March 1966 Ali received a notice from the draft board to report for duty in the Army. With the Vietnam War raging, Ali refused to serve. His boxing license was revoked in every state. Four years later the Atlanta Athletic Commission reinstated his license and Ali stepped into the ring against Jerry Quarry which he won. His professional record is 56 wins, 5 losses.

In 1996 in Atlanta, Ali was given the honor of lighting the Olympic torch to start the games. In declining health and suffering from Parkinson's Disease, "The Greatest" died June 3, 2016.

National Association for the Advancement of Colored People

Founded in 1909 by a group of white liberals like Mary White Ovington, Oswald Garrison Villard, William English Wailing, seven blacks including W.E.B. DuBois, Ida B. Wells Mary Church Terrell, a number of prominent Jews, Dr. Henry Moscowitz, Joel and Arthur Spingarn and Lillian Wald and 50 others.

It was created to address the problems of lynching and violence against blacks, to promote equal protection of the law and eliminate racial prejudice.

DuBose began publishing "The Crisis" a magazine promoting black art, writing and poetry. It was instrumental in spotlighting black creativity during the Harlem Renaissance. It's still being published today.

By 1913 branch offices were opened in major cities. Membership increased from 9.000 in 1917 to 90,000 two years later.

With wins in the courts and strong leadership the NAACP grew more powerful. Some major victories include the desegregation of the military by President Harry Truman; *Brown v Board of Education*, argued in the U.S. Supreme Court by Thurgood Marshall and the outlawing of job discrimination in the armed forces, defense industries and federal agencies by President Franklin D. Roosevelt.

During the Civil Rights Era the NAACP provided legal representation and posted bail for Freedom Riders who had traveled to the south to register voters.

The NAACP, the oldest civil rights organization in the country, continues to fight against racial inequality, voter suppression and discrimination in education, health care, economics and wherever there's injustice.

Nellie Stone Johnson

Nellie Stone Johnson was born December 12, 1905 in Minnesota's Dakota County. Her parents were supporters of racial and religious tolerance.

She moved to Minneapolis to finish high school and was hired as an elevator operator where she experienced discrimination and workers who weren't union members. She believed education and union membership provided a better life for African-Americans.

When the National Labor Relations Act was passed in 1935, she began organizing workers at downtown hotels and restaurants. The resulting unions won wage increases and uniform job descriptions through collective bargaining.

She was the first woman vice-president of the Minnesota Culinary Council and the first woman vice-president of Local 665, Hotel and Restaurant Employees Union. She was also elected to the city Library Board in 1945, the first black person elected to citywide office.

She owned and operated Nellie's Alterations in downtown Minneapolis for more than 30 years.

She received many awards including one from the W. Harry Davis Foundation for her service to the community. An educational fund, the "Nellie Stone Johnson Scholarship" was founded in 1989 and she was given an honorary doctorate degree from St. Cloud State University.

She continued her involvement in the NAACP, the National Council of Negro Women and the Urban League.

She died in Minneapolis April 2, 2002 at age 96.

The Orangeburg Massacre

On February 6, 1968 a group of black students went to the segregated All-Star Bowling Alley in Orangeburg, South Carolina and sat at the counter waiting to be served. They were protesting at one of the last segregated businesses in town.

On the second night more students from South Carolina State College, a predominantly black school, joined the protest and 15 were arrested. During the melee nine students and one city policeman were injured.

Tensions were high on the third day of protests, February 8. Due to freezing temperatures, students lit a bonfire on the street in front of the school just off campus. A firetruck was called to douse the fire and state police arrived. The troopers, all white, had little or no training in crowd control. They moved to protect the fire fighters while more than 100 students retreated to the campus.

A bannister thrown from a window hit a state trooper who fell to the ground bleeding. Soon after, about 70 law enforcement officers lined the edge of the campus armed with an assortment of weapons.

A patrolman fired a few shots from his carbine into the air, intended as warning shots. Hearing the gunfire, other officers opened fire on the crowd. The fleeing students were shot in the back or on the bottom of their feet as they ran.

Samuel Hammond, Henry Smith and Delano Middleton died that night and 27 others were wounded.

More than a year later, a federal court jury acquitted the nine troopers charged in the case.

In 1970, a jury in Orangeburg convicted SNCC representative Cleveland Sellers, Jr. of inciting the riot that led to the shootings. He served seven months of a one-year sentence.

Paul Robeson

Robeson was born April 9, 1898. His mother, Anna Louisa, died in a fire when he was six years old.

In school he was an excellent athlete and he sang in the church choir. When he was 17, he earned a scholarship to Rutgers University. While there he excelled in his studies and was recognized for his debate and oratory skills. He also won 15 letters in four varsity sports.

Robeson earned a degree from Columbia University School of Law and upon graduation joined a law firm only to leave when racial tension grew unbearable. In order to pay for tuition, he played pro football on weekends and taught Latin. He would eventually learn and speak 15 languages.

Using his public speaking skills, he sought employment as an actor, playing the lead in two Eugene O'Neill plays, *"All God's Chillun Got Wings"* and *"The Emperor Jones."* The role for which he's most famous is that of Joe, the stevedore in the 1936 musical, *"Showboat"* where he sings "Ol' Man River" which became his signature song.

Widely popular internationally he regularly spoke out against racial injustice and other causes. He often visited the Soviet Union intrigued by Russian folk culture and where he was treated with respect not found at home.

During a period called the "Cold War," with tensions rising between Russia and the United States over Communism vs. Capitalism, Wisconsin Senator Joseph McCarthy accused Robeson of being an anti-American Communist. Robeson was blacklisted and his passport revoked.

No longer able to continue his career, he became severely depressed and retired from performing. He died in Philadelphia, Pennsylvania of a stroke on January 23, 1976 and the age of 77.

Quincy Jones, Jr.

Jones was born March 14, 1933 in Chicago, Illinois.

Ten years later the family moved to Bremerton, Washington and then to the city of Seattle. In high school, Jones played the trumpet and did some musical arranging.

He joined the Lionel Hampton band as a trumpet player and arranger. When he left the band in 1953, he started to arrange music for Count Basie, Sarah Vaughn, Dinah Washington, Tommy Dorsey and Ray Charles.

He was named vice president of Mercury Records in 1961, the first African-American to hold an executive position in a white-owned business.

Sidney Lumet, the director of the movie *"The Pawnbroker,"* asked him to write music for the movie. More offers followed with Jones composing music for *"Mirage"* and *"The Slender Thread."*

During the 1960's Jones produced records for Leslie Gore. He also produced albums for some of the top-named stars in music.

In 1985 he brought together some of the biggest musical stars at the time to record, *"We are the World,"* a fundraising album to aid the victims of famine in Ethiopia.

He produced some of the greatest albums of Michael Jackson, including the mega-hit, "Thriller."

His social activism is evident in his support of the NAACP and as a founder of the Institute for Black American Music whose purpose is to raise money to create a library of African-American art and music.

Ralph Bunche

Born August 7, 1904, he was to become one of the most notable diplomats in America and around the world.

Raised by his grandmother after his parents died, he excelled in school and in sports graduating summa cum laude from UCLA in 1927.

Always an advocate of civil rights he was a consultant on minority problems in the Roosevelt administration. Because of the segregated housing in the nation's capital he declined an appointment by President Truman to be Assistant Secretary of State.

Bunche also helped organize the march from Selma to Montgomery, Alabama in 1965 and was a supporter of the NAACP and the Urban League.

His prominence as a diplomat came as a member of the United Nations whose charter he helped create. In1946, Trygve Lie, then Secretary-General of the U.N. put Bunche in charge of a committee to aid people who had not achieved self-government.

In 1948, when Israel was declared a Jewish state, the surrounding Arab states declared war against the new country. Bunche was sent to negotiate an armistice agreement, which was successful. The NAACP awarded him the Spingarn Prize in 1949 and a year later he was awarded the Nobel Peace Prize.

From 1955 to 1967, Bunche was Undersecretary for Special Political Affairs and in 1968 he became Undersecretary-General of the United Nations. He was instrumental in assigning U.N. peacekeeping forces to areas of conflict throughout the world.

Ralph Bunche died December 9, 1971 from kidney and heart disease.

Ralph David Abernathy, Sr.

Abernathy was the 10th of 12 children and was born March 11, 1926 in Linden, Alabama on the family's 500-acre farm.

He became an ordained minister in 1948 and was the pastor of the First Baptist Church in Montgomery, Alabama.

In 1954, Martin Luther King became the minister of a nearby church and the two formed a life-long bond.

After Rosa Parks was arrested for refusing to give up her seat on the bus to a white rider, the two men formed the Montgomery Improvement Association and organized a year-long boycott of the bus system. He was also active in the NAACP and became chairman of the Baptist Training Union Congress' committee on the Brown v. Board of Education ruling desegregating public schools.

In 1957 he and King formed the Southern Christian Leadership Conference with King as president and, eventually, Abernathy as vice president. The SCLC became the premier civil rights organization in the south.

Upon King's recommendation, Abernathy was hired as pastor of the West Hunter Baptist Church in Atlanta in1961. The two friends were able to lend support to each other while continuing to pursue civil rights for African-Americans. Many times, that meant defying authority. They were jailed together 17 times for disobedience.

When Martin Luther King was assassinated on April 4, 1968, Abernathy took over the SCLC as its president. He continued King's plan to support the Memphis sanitation workers and organized the Poor People's Campaign to Washington, D. C.

In 1977 he unsuccessfully ran for a seat in Congress.

He died April 17, 1990 in Atlanta.

Robert Smalls

Robert Smalls was born into slavery on April 5, 1839 in Beaufort, South Carolina.

His mother made sure he worked in the fields so he could see first-hand the abuse suffered by other slaves. It had a profound effect on young Robert.

Fearing for his safety she asked plantation owner John McKee to allow Smalls to be rented out to work in Charleston.

By the time he was 19 he was an expert in navigating Charleston harbor.

For a long time, he worked on the *C.S.S. Planter*, a ship that hauled cotton, owned by Capt. C. J. Relyea. The captain's trust in Smalls was so strong that on the night of May 13, 1862, the captain and his small crew left Smalls in charge and went ashore. Smalls had been waiting for just this moment.

Wearing the captain's hat and hoisting the correct flags, the *Planter* eased away from the dock. They paused at a wharf to pick up Small's wife and children and friends then sailed toward the Union fleet blockading Charleston harbor. He had to pass through many checkpoints but he used the ship's horn to sound the correct signals. Safely out of range of Confederate guns, Smalls raised a white bed sheet and surrendered the ship. All aboard the *Planter* were now free.

On April 7, 1863 he piloted the "Keokuk" as it and eight other ironclads sailed into Charleston to demand the surrender of the city.

Smalls was elected to the South Carolina state assembly and the Senate. He also served five terms as a member of the U.S. House of Representatives.

He died in Beaufort February 22, 1915.

Rosa Parks

Called the *"Mother of the Civil Rights Movement,"* Rosa Parks was born February 4, 1913 in Tuskegee, Alabama.

When she was two years old, she and her family moved to her grandparent's farm where she enrolled in school at age 11.

In 1932 she married Raymond Parks, a barber and a member of the NAACP in Montgomery, Alabama. She joined the chapter too and became its secretary.

On December 1, 1955, Parks was sitting in the black section of a bus in Montgomery on her way home from work. There were no more seats in the white section when white riders boarded the bus. James F. Blake, the bus driver told four black passengers, Parks included, to give up their seats. Three of the others complied. Rosa Parks said, "No." The driver had her arrested.

News of her arrest spread throughout the city. NAACP members gathered to plan the next move. 35,000 flyers were distributed throughout Montgomery urging blacks to boycott the buses. Word was passed through the black churches and word-of-mouth. What began as a one-day boycott, the day of Parks' trial, eventually became one which lasted 381 days. The NAACP elected a 26-year-old minister, a newcomer to the city, named Martin Luther King, to manage the boycott.

Anger among whites resulted in the bombing of black homes and businesses. The court appeals and lawsuits eventually made their way to the U.S. Supreme Court which ruled, on November 13, 1965, that bus segregation was unconstitutional.

After losing her job as a department store seamstress she was hired by Congressman John Conyers as his secretary. She died October 24, 2005 at the age of 92.

Roy Campanella

He became a catcher on his high school baseball team because no one else wanted the job and he wanted to play the game.

Hall of Famer Roy Campanella was born on the 19th of November, 1921 in Homestead, Pennsylvania.

"Campy" was 15 when he dropped out of school to play professional baseball with the Bacharach Giants in Brooklyn, New York.

He played nine years in the Negro Leagues sometimes playing four games in a single day. His salary was $3,000 a season. He learned to live and play with pain since players didn't get paid if they didn't play.

He was signed by Branch Rickey, the Brooklyn Dodgers president, who sent him to the minor leagues in Nashua, New Hampshire. Campanella soon became one of the team's best players.

He played 113 games with the Nashua Dodgers compiling a .290 batting average. He was then sent to the Class AAA team in Montreal, Canada where he was behind the plate for 135 games.

Rickey brought "Campy" to the major leagues in 1948; a year after Jackie Robinson joined the club. He became one of the best hitting catchers in baseball. He was a three-time National League Most Valuable Player and he played in eight All-Star games.

He was instrumental in the Brooklyn Dodgers only World Series title in 1955 over the New York Yankees.

His career ended in 1958 when he was paralyzed in an automobile accident.

He was inducted into the Baseball Hall of Fame in 1969.

Roy Wilkins

Born in St. Louis, Missouri August 30,1901, Wilkins grew up in a poor, integrated community in St. Paul, Minnesota.

He graduated from the University of Minnesota in1923 with a degree in sociology.

Early in his career he was a newspaper reporter for the *"Kansas City Call,"* a publication serving the African-American community.

Wilkins, Arnold Aronson, a leader of the National Jewish Community Relations Advisory Council and A. Philip Randolph, founder of the Brotherhood of Sleeping Car Porters organized the Leadership Conference on Civil Rights in1950.

Five years later Wilkins was named Executive Director of the NAACP, a post he held until he retired in1977.

During the early years of the civil rights struggle, Wilkins looked to the courts to fight for equal rights. He was able to testify before Congressional committees and was an advisor to five presidents: John F. Kennedy, Lyndon Johnson, Richard Nixon, Gerald Ford and Jimmy Carter.

He was also able to convince black businesses and voluntary organizations in Mound Bayou, Mississippi to take their money from white owned banks, where it was difficult for blacks to get loans, to the black-owned Tri-State Bank which did extend loans to credit-worthy black citizens.

He helped organize the historic March on Washington in 1963. Hundreds of thousands of people came to the Lincoln Memorial to hear speeches by Wilkins and others. At this event Dr. Martin Luther King gave his "I Have a Dream" speech.

In 1967 President Lyndon Johnson awarded him the Presidential Medal of Freedom. He died September 8, 1981.

Shirley Chisholm

A strong, combative woman who fought for her constituents while in Congress, Chisholm was a child of immigrants.

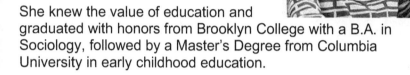

She was born in Brooklyn, N. Y. on November 20, 1924. Her father was a factory worker from Guyana and her mother was a seamstress from Barbados.

She knew the value of education and graduated with honors from Brooklyn College with a B.A. in Sociology, followed by a Master's Degree from Columbia University in early childhood education.

When a new congressional district was created in her neighborhood of Bedford-Stuyvesant she ran for the office and defeated James Farmer, a co-founder of CORE, the Congress of Racial Equality. The victory made her the first African-American woman in Congress.

She was outspoken on the issues of the day from her first days in the House of Representatives which didn't endear her to the House leadership. She was initially assigned to the Agriculture Committee but soon after was given a spot on the Veterans Affairs Committee.

In 1972 she declared her candidacy for president of the United States because no other candidate was representing blacks and the poor. She appeared on a dozen primary ballots. At the Democratic National Convention, she received 151 votes from delegates, a respectable showing even though she didn't win the nomination.

She retired from the House in 1982 after serving 14 years.

President Bill Clinton nominated her as ambassador to Jamaica which she refused due to declining health. She died January 1, 2005.

Sidney Poitier

Poitier was born February 20, 1924 in Miami, Florida. For most of his youth he lived in the Bahamas.

His family was extremely poor and at age 15 he went to live with his brother in Miami.

Three years later he moved to New York City. While working at various menial jobs he auditioned at the American Negro Theatre and was promptly thrown out. His accent and poor reading skills proved to be a disadvantage. Six months later, having improved both skills he was hired by the theatre.

A casting director noticed him on stage and gave him a small part In the Broadway production of "Lysistrata." After accepting other roles, he was cast as a doctor in the film, *"No Way Out"* in 1950. He played different characters in the films that followed: *"Cry the Beloved Country," "Blackboard Jungle"* and *"The Defiant Ones,"* which earned him an Academy Award nomination.

In 1963 he won the Best Actor Award, the Oscar, for the film *"lilies in the Field,"* the first black actor to win in that category. Also, that year he joined Dr. Martin Luther King, Jr. on the march from Selma to Montgomery, Alabama.

As an actor he's taken roles in some classic movies: *"To Sir, With Love," "In the Heat of the Night"* and *"Guess Who's Coming to Dinner."* Poitier has also won acclaim as a film director.

He's been the recipient of many awards including the Screen Actors Guild Lifetime Achievement Award, the NAACP's Hall of Fame Award, a Grammy Award for reading his autobiography and an honorary Academy Award for his many achievements in film.

Student Non-Violent Coordinating Committee

When four black college students were denied service at a Woolworth's lunch counter in Greensboro, N.C. they stayed until the store closed. The "sit-in" movement spread throughout the south protesting racial discrimination.

Ella Baker, an official with the NAACP held a conference at Shaw University in Raleigh, N.C. and organized the Student Non-Violent Coordinating Committee (SNCC). Its first president was Marion Berry, later to be elected mayor of Washington, D.C.

"Snick" as it became known, concentrated on sit-ins at lunch counters but soon expanded its efforts to include voter registration.

During the summer of 1964, "Freedom Summer," hundreds of black and white college students volunteered to join Mississippi SNCC workers and local civil rights activists to register black voters. They were highly successful and received national notoriety.

The successful registration drive was marred by the disappearance of three workers. The bodies of James E. Chaney of Mississippi, Michael H. Schwerner and Andrew Goodman of New York were found 44 days later near Philadelphia, Mississippi. They had been murdered by white supremacists.

John Lewis, who was chairman of SNCC, was replaced by Stokely Carmichael in May 1966. He believed a more radical approach was needed by the organization and when H. Rap Brown became chairman the following year the radicalization and anti-white sentiment increased.

With the expulsion of whites, SNCC's annual income dropped and programs were scaled back. Soon after, its employees left and in December 1973 the organization ceased to exist.

Sojourner Truth

Her real name was Isabella Baumfree and she was born in a Dutch settlement in upstate New York in 1797, one of 13 children.

She was sold as a slave when she was nine years old. In 1810 she was sold again to John Dumont of New Paltz, New York where she was abused by Mrs. Dumont.

She escaped from the Dumont's and after wandering arrived at the home of Isaac and Maria Van Wagenen. During her time with the Van Wagenen's she became inspired to preach and she quickly became an influential preacher.

At the time of her escape she left behind her children with the exception of Sophia, her infant daughter. She found out her five-year-old son, Isaac, had been sold illegally to a new master in Alabama by John Dumont. With the help of the Wagenen's she went to court to gain custody of him. In 1828 the court found in her favor. Truth became one of the first black women to win a court case against a white man.

On June1, 1843 she changed her name to Sojourner Truth because "the spirit called me," she said.

A year later she joined the Northampton Association of Education and Industry which was founded by abolitionists. The organization supported women's rights and religious tolerance. It was there she met Frederick Douglass and others.

In 1851 while attending the Ohio Women's Rights Convention she gave her most famous speech, "Ain't I a Woman?"

In 1864 she went to Washington, D. C. to help integrate street cars and while there met President Lincoln.

Sojourner Truth died November 26, 1883 at the age of 86.

Thurgood Marshall

Marshall was the first African-American to serve on the Supreme Court of the United States.

Born in Baltimore, Maryland July 2,1908, this son of a railroad porter and a school teacher would become a major figure in the struggle for civil rights.

One of his first legal victories was "Murray v. Patterson" in1935. He successfully sued the University of Maryland for denying an African-American student admittance to their law school based solely on race.

By1938 he had become the chief of the NAACP Legal Defense and Education Fund. He travelled around the country representing clients affected by racial injustice.

He argued thirty-two cases before the U.S. Supreme Court winning twenty-nine of them. His most notable case is "Brown v. Board of Education." It was a case which challenged racial segregation in public schools. The court sided with Marshall citing that segregated schools supposedly having equal resources (separate but equal) was not applicable to public education because it could never be truly equal.

President John Kennedy appointed Marshall to the U.S. Court of Appeals for the Second Circuit in1961. A group of southern senators held up his nomination but he was eventually confirmed and remained on the court until1965.

President Lyndon Johnson nominated him to the U.S. Supreme Court on June 13, 1967 and he was confirmed by the Senate that August. He served on the court for 24 years.

Marshall retired from the Supreme Court in1991 and died two years later.

Tuskegee Airmen

Tuskegee fighter pilots take a break between missions

World War 2 began in Europe in 1939 when Germany invaded Czechoslovakia.

U. S. President Franklin D. Roosevelt, seeing the possibility of America's entry expanded the Army Air Corps to recruit pilots.

In 1940, despite racial segregation in America, and after extensive lobbying, Roosevelt opened the AAC to train black pilots.

They were headquartered at Tuskegee Institute, founded by Booker T. Washington, because it had an air field.

Thousands of potential recruits from across the nation answered the call, among them Benjamin O. Davis, Jr. who became the first black general officer in the Air Force.

In 1942 the Tuskegee Airmen became the 99th Pursuit Squadron, an all-black unit, which was deployed to North Africa then Sicily. They flew second-hand P-40 aircraft which weren't as good as the German airplanes.

In 1944 the group merged with others to become the 332nd Fighter Group. They now flew P-51 Mustangs while escorting bombers on their missions deep into enemy territory. The tails of their planes were painted red to distinguish them from others. They became known as the "Red Tails."

Nine hundred ninety-two pilots were trained at Tuskegee from 1941 to 1946. They excelled in their escort duties flying 179 missions losing only 25 bombers during the war. Three Distinguished Unit Citations were awarded their unit. Personal awards included 96 Distinguished Flying Crosses, 744 Air Medals, 14 Bronze Stars, 8 Purple Hearts and at least one Silver Star.

W.E.B. DuBois

William Edward Burkhardt DuBois was born February 23, 1868 in Great Barrington, Massachusetts. He was a good student and became valedictorian of his senior class.

Wanting to attend Harvard, but lacking the funds, he attended Fisk College in Nashville where he witnessed discrimination and vowed to work to end it. When he graduated from Fisk, he was able, through scholarships, to attend Harvard University where he studied philosophy, economics and social problems. He became the first African-American to earn a Ph.D. at Harvard.

In 1896 he accepted a fellowship at the University of Pennsylvania to study African-American urban life. His book, "The Philadelphia Negro" suggested housing and discrimination in employment were the major causes of racial inequality and the lack of black prosperity in the north.

In 1909, DuBois joined Ida B. Wells, five other blacks and 53 white liberals in forming the NAACP. He edited the group's magazine, "The Crisis," for 25 years.

He eventually left the NAACP because of the continuation of white racism and what he considered the condescension of black leaders.

During the "cold war" DuBois tried to broker a peace. A controversial move, it came to the attention of the F.B.I. The State Department revoked his passport.

Embracing the Communist Party which, he said, was the only hope for working class people and the only way racism could be defeated, he gave up his U. S. citizenship and moved to the African country of Ghana.

He died August 27, 1963, on the eve of the March on Washington.

Walter Francis White

White was born July 1, 1893 in the city of Atlanta, Georgia and was so light-skinned he could have "passed" for white. He used that anomaly to infiltrate white supremacy groups to learn first-hand their involvement with lynchings and racial violence.

In 1916 he became one of the founders of the Atlanta chapter of the NAACP and two years later joined the organization as assistant secretary. In 1929 he became head of the NAACP.

In 1941 he helped persuade President Franklin D. Roosevelt to prohibit racial discrimination in defense industries. Roosevelt made it law through his executive order 8802 which also established the Fair Employment Practices Commission to monitor compliance of anti-discrimination legislation.

Under his stewardship the NAACP was able to successfully lobby against a Supreme Court nominee who opposed the right of blacks to vote. He was also able to convince President Harry Truman to create a civil rights commission. He invited Truman to speak to the NAACP's annual convention, which the president did.

White authored a number of books based on his experiences. *"Fire in the Flint,"* published in 1924 and *"Flight"* published two years later were novels. *"Rope and Faggot,"* dealt with lynchings. His other works included, *"A Rising Wind," "A Man called White,"* and *"How far the Promised Land?"*

Walter White died in New York City in 1955.

On February 21, 2009, the United States Postal Service honored him and 11 other civil rights pioneers with the issuance of six 42-cent first class commemorative stamps.

Whitney Young Jr.

Young was born July 31, 1921 in Lincoln
Ridge, Kentucky. His father was the principal
of the Lincoln Institute, a preparatory school for
African-Americans. His mother was a teacher.

He became a teacher after graduation from
Kentucky State Industrial College. He also
served in World War II.

In 1947 he began working for the National Urban League's
Minnesota chapter and later became president of the chapter in
Omaha, Nebraska where he expanded membership in the
organization.

As civil rights became a national issue, Young helped blacks get
jobs in the community.

He pressured Ford Motor Company and other industries to hire
more African-Americans and he created programs to lower high
school dropout rates.

In 1963 the Urban League, at Young's insistence, co-sponsored
the March on Washington.

He was an advisor to three presidents: John F. Kennedy, Lyndon
B. Johnson and Richard Nixon. He was even mentioned as a
candidate for a cabinet post in the Nixon administration.

With the Vietnam War raging, which he eventually opposed,
Young established a veteran's affairs department for the Urban
League.

He received the Presidential Medal of Freedom Award from
Lyndon Johnson in 1968 for his ground-breaking efforts on behalf
of civil rights.

Young was attending a conference in Lagos, Nigeria when he died
in 1971. The cause has never been confirmed. He was 49 years
old.

Attributions

Alvin Ailey Library of Congress, Prints & Photographs Division, Carl Van Vechten Collection, [reproduction number, e.g. LC-USZ62-54231} (lots 12735 & 12736)

Amelia Boynton Robinson   Photo by Jamelle Bouie, https://flickr.com/photos/40050039@N2/7946362634

Arthur Ashe Bob Bogaerts/anefo.item#927-7839 (and/or) thekojonnamdishow.org/shows/2014/09/08/Arthur-ashe

Benjamin Mays RobertTempleton.com/myportfolio/Benjamin-mays

Bernard Lafayette Photo credit: The University of Michigan – Flint

Billie Holiday Library of Congress, Prints & Photographs Division, Carl Van Vechten Collection (lots 12735 & 12736)

Booker T. Washington Portrait by Frances Benjamin Johnston

Charles Drew Portrait by Betsy Graves Reyneau

Diane Nash Germanna CC at https://flickr.com/photos/61150757@N02/15542299001

Dick Gregory John Matthew Smith & www.celebrity-photos.com at https://flickr.com/photos/36277035@N06/5113177828

Ethel Waters Library of Congress, Prints & Photographs Division, Carl Van Vechten Collection (Lots 12735 & 12736)

Fred Shuttlesworth World Telegram & Sun

Gwendolyn Brooks World Telegram & Sun

Harry Truman World Telegram & Sun

James Baldwin Library of Congress, Prints & Photographs Division, Carl Van Vechten Collection (lots 12735 & 12736)

Jesse Jackson Flickr.com/photos/afge/10196156245

Joseph Lowery John Matthew Smith & www.celebrity-photos.com at https://flickr.com/photos/36277035@N06/39897479403

Josephine Baker Library of Congress, Prints & Photographs Division, Carl Van Vechten Collection (lots 12735 & 12736)

Leontyne Price Library of Congress, Prints & Photographs Division, Carl Van Vechten Collection (lots 12735 & 12736)

Martin Luther King World Telegram & Sun

Mary McLeod Bethune Library of Congress, Prints & Photographs Division, Carl Van Vechten Collection (lots 12735 & 12736)

Maya Angelou John Matthew Smith & www.celebrity-photos.com at https://flickr.com/photos/36277035@N06/47327455761

Muhammad Ali Kingkongphoto&www.celebrity-photos.com at https://flickr.com/photos/36277035@N06/5112586507

Nellie Stone Johnson WorkdayMinnesota.org/labor-civil-rights-leader-nellie-stone-johnson-dies

Ralph Bunche Library of Congress, Prints & Photographs Division, Carl Van Vechten Collection (lots 12735 & 12736)

W. E. B. DuBose National Park Service

All others: Library of Congress or Wikimediacommons

Tuskegee Airmen: Left to right – Lt. Dempsey W. Morgan, Jr.; Lt Carroll S. Woods; Lt. Robert H. Nelson, Jr.; Capt. Andrew D. Turner and Lt. Clarence Lester (1944)

CPSIA information can be obtained
at www.ICGtesting.com
Printed in the USA
LVHW090757181119
637663LV00012B/5275/P